NEVER FINISHED

Never Finished

Practical advice for Modern Women to inspire your fierce, authentic self

JILL D. MILLER

Finishing School for Modern Women

For more information or to book an event, contact jill@finish-ingschoolformodernwomen.com.

Creative Solutions
1999 N. Amidon, Suite 370
Wichita, KS 67204
First Printing, 2022

Book design by Jessica Wasson-Crook

This book is dedicated to all the Modern Women who
chase their dreams while trying to stay positive,
fight demons,
find or sustain love,
keep in touch with friends and family,
heal from past trauma,
break generational curses,
all while finding time to enjoy life while we have it.

Contents

Introduction

I started the Finishing School for Modern Women in 2015, but I'd been planning it much longer than that. Since I was a little bitty red-headed girl, I knew I wanted to be an entrepreneur. I didn't have any idea what kind of business I'd start. I just knew that I was going to be the boss.

I took all the business classes I could in junior high and high school, but in the mid-'70s, these classes were all about preparing women to work in the secretarial pool.

The idea that we could use these skills to be a business mogul was considered ludicrous then. We were in training to be nurses, secretaries, sales clerks, bookkeepers, waitresses, teachers, and of course, moms. Professional positions for women were still considered ambitious, which isn't surprising since a woman couldn't even have a credit card under her name until 1974.

I knew my life would be different when I grew up. Rather than typing letters for someone else, I would have an office downtown with my own secretary.

But, if it weren't for the women's liberation movement, I might not have realized that being a Boss Lady was possible. So when Helen Reddy's big hit, "I Am Woman," came out in 1972, I proudly sang along with this anthem that influenced many lives.

I have now realized my entrepreneurial dream with a secretary and office downtown. In 1998 I started Creative Solutions, a business development consulting practice. For nearly 25 years, I've helped women and creatives start and grow their business ownership aspirations, some into multi-million-dollar businesses.

I learned a lot about running a small business while managing a creative and chaotic hair salon during the wild 1980s. And more about what not to do. I had a decade of experience, a passion for the beauty industry, and a love of people. I left the salon and went to work for the distributor of Aveda products, one of the brands we carried in the salon. I fell in love with their product, mission, and company.

Aveda's philosophy was so much more than selling products. They were changing the world through environmental steward-ship in manufacturing their products. They were also making the salon business environment healthier by teaching business owners how to implement business systems and run more successful companies.

Salon owners are usually talented artists with a passion for the industry but little business experience. I did hours and hours of in-salon training that went beyond product knowl-edge. I taught stylists how to sell, stand out in the market, enhance customer service, and improve team culture. I knew if I could help the salon professionals I worked with grow, I would be more successful.

I learned from my work in the salon world that what I love best is teaching and helping people grow. The irony of such a traditionally female role is not lost on me. But, it is in my ancestry. I come from a long line of teachers, so it really shouldn't be a surprise that public speaking comes naturally to me. Every business idea I've ever had included an education component to the plan. Coming to that realization has helped me understand how to progress.

Part of my consulting practice has always included corporate training. I've traveled near and far, giving classes to companies of all sizes and industries. I've taught Entrepreneurship in the Arts for the school of Fine Arts at Wichita State University since 2014, and I love helping these students be strategic in how they look at making a living doing what they love.

In 2014, my life took a sudden turn. After 24 years of marriage, I realized that the unhealthy parts of the relationship would never change, and it was up to me to stop the madness. I left and never looked back, putting me at one of those life crossroads. I had to figure out how to reinvent my life and heal from the past trauma to build a brilliant future. While I continued my consulting practice, I started thinking about what that might look like.

Previously I read *"Radiating Like a Stone, Wichita Women, and the 1970s Feminist Movement,"* an anthology of essays about local women who fought hard for women's equality. I realized that many of the same issues that held women back then still held us back. Frustrated by this, I thought, "How can this happen? How do we keep the momentum going?" I started thinking about how I could accomplish this on my own and lead others to this same idea.

My hero, Myrne Roe, the editor of
Radiating Like a Stone

As I started researching my next big move, I read *"Playing Big,"* a book by Tara Mohr. This book is about how women hold themselves back in business, a dilemma I've seen many times in my consulting practice. This book pointed out that it's up to every one of us to make changes, starting with ourselves.

I started planning the Finishing School for Modern Women in the summer of 2015 and put together an advisory panel of 80 women. I held several focus groups, getting advice on what to charge, what classes sounded interesting, and how to make it fun. The first class on September 19, 2015, "Keep Moving Forward," at Harvester Arts, was a big success, with 25 attending.

The first Finishing School for Modern
Women class

I continued to give classes at Harvester Arts, the Wichita Art Museum, and Watermark Books and Café for the rest of 2015, using that time as a test period to see if there was enough interest and demand to continue. Thanks to the people who attended and co-taught classes those first couple of months, I decided there was a need for the kind of classes we offer and that I had found my mission in life. Deciding to go all in, I opened a storefront at 340 S. Main in March 2016.

Then the COVID pandemic happened, changing how we're doing classes at the Finishing School for Modern Women forever. We offered live classes online and in-person simultaneously so everyone could play.

I liked the juxtaposition between what finishing schools once were, compared to what women need now, not because we need finishing, but because we're never finished. We offer a wide variety of classes based on feminine perspectives, all with a creative twist. While the classes are designed for women, all genders are welcome at the Finishing School for Modern Women.

Our co-teachers are experts in their field and include therapists, career counselors, organizational specialists, and other professionals. Classes are interactive and discussion-based to keep things fun and interesting, using adult learning techniques to make the experience more meaningful. Each class has an icon we make into collectible "badges" awarded at a graduation ceremony at the end of class.

These are not your grandmother's etiquette classes. My goal in the Finishing School for Modern Women is to empower women of all ages to come together to learn from each other through open, candid conversations. To pass on the skills, women need to claim their power to live a happier and more successful life. To help women realize more confidence through knowledge that comes from community and shared experiences. To inspire Modern Women to realize their fierce, authentic selves and never stop the search for self-realization.

This book was inspired by some of the contents of my blogs over the past seven years on https://www.finishingschoolformodernwomen.com. Check the back of this book to find out how to join us.

Thank you for helping make this dream come true,

Headmistress Jill

Chapter One

Never Finish Discovering

How We Treat Ourselves

1. Love Yourself

2. True Beauty

3. Body Acceptance Tips

4. No Shame

5. Sparkle

6. Finding Your Purpose

7. Let it Shine

Love Yourself

My man Jack is the best company

I've been single for several years now, and I'm more than okay with that. I did the math and figured out that I've been paired up 87 percent of my adult life, so taking some time to be untethered isn't the end of the world. This time by myself has freed me up to explore who I am.

Like any relationship, improving my connection with myself took work. The Finishing School for Modern Women classes are undoubtedly part of this journey. Especially in the beginning, many of the classes I created were on topics I struggled with or wanted to explore. Researching and writing classes helped me better understand who I was and how I wanted to reinvent myself. Talking with other Modern Women in class always gives me clarity and helps me realize that I'm never really alone in what I'm thinking and experiencing.

I'm never truly alone in many other aspects of my life too. I have an incredible support network with a loving family, dedicated friends, and Jack, my loneliness therapy poodle. I'm also fortunate to have a fantastic therapist I've worked with off and on for 90 percent of my adult life, who helps give me the insight to heal past traumas and build resilience to avoid new ones.

At first, the most challenging aspect of being single was feeling like no one had my back. I felt all alone. I especially missed having an easily accessible sounding board to discuss what I was thinking and working on, help me make big decisions, or give me a reality check. But, I've found many people in my life who could fill this gap. I just had to reach out.

I've been reflecting on what it means to be single lately. Of course, Valentine's Day always spurs those thoughts in us single ladies, but this year it also hit me that an important anniversary was approaching. Last week, it was five years since I decided to end my 24-year marriage and flee my husband.

It was the hardest decision I've ever made and not one I took lightly. It took me seven years to work up the nerve and own up to the fact that things would never get better and were increasingly getting worse. It was hard to take a leap of faith to turn my life upside down and start over again, but I did it!

Even though it was tough, it was the best decision I've ever made. Taking that action put me on the path of falling in love with who I am. I'm not saying it's easy to break free because it's been one of my biggest life challenges. But the reinvention has been worth the struggle. Since the only relationship we'll have throughout our entire lifetime is with ourselves, we better make that relationship the best it can be.

My friend Marva posted something that caught my attention on Facebook. She was cleaning her house and found a broken bowl that she'd been keeping. She didn't want to throw it away because it was a wedding present she had bought when marrying herself, vowing that she'd never leave herself for anyone else again. I understood precisely what she was talking about. It's too easy to leave ourselves when we're partnered up. I've compromised too much of myself in the past and don't want to do that again. It made me wonder what my wedding vows would be to myself. What would yours be?

It isn't easy to learn to love ourselves, despite our obvious flaws. Here are some strategies that have helped me, and naturally, I'm willing to share my secrets with you.

Pay attention to the "Joy Suck" rule.

For many years I've tried to live by the rule that if something is sucking the joy out of my life, it's got to go. This gets especially hard when it's someone you love. Prioritizing our love for ourselves before anything else makes the action we need to take obvious. Life is too short to be miserable, and if something is sucking the joy out of our life, you can change it. You owe that to yourself.

Learn to be comfortable with being uncomfortable.

When the worst thing I can imagine happens in my life, it always amazes me that it turns out not to be the worst thing that could happen. It often means I get new coping skills or that something new opens up in the place of what's gone, or that I get to reinvent myself to make my life even better than it was before. Desperately holding on to the status quo, so I didn't have to feel uncomfortable for a shortish time was killing my potential for overall happiness.

Tell yourself, "I love you."

One day it dawned on me – I tell people I love them all the time, but when was the last time I said that to myself? Since that day, I look myself in the eyes in the mirror at least once a day, when I'm putting on makeup or doing my hair, and tell myself, "I love you." At first, it was a bit uncomfortable, but the way it has affected my attitude is profound.

Change how you listen to love songs.

At one of the saddest times in my life, I was driving down the street when a love song came over the radio. I can't remember what the song was, but I remember thinking, "This is a love song from me – to me." Since that time, I have listened to love songs differently. Music is incredibly healing. Songs like "I Will Survive" by Gloria Gaynor have been a healing anthem in my life more than once, and "Stand" by Sly and Family Stone always gives me strength.

Work on resting happy face.

Resting happy face is something new I'm trying. We've all heard of "resting bitch face," when we tend to look perturbed when we're just relaxing. I've decided to try "resting happy face." Whenever I think about it, I try to slightly turn up the corners of my mouth and smile rather than automatically having a slack expression on my face. I'm amazed at how it makes me feel. Just smiling raises my spirits.

Build your support network.

Many people latch onto one poor soul for their sole support. Instead, spread the love around and pick a whole team of people based on their strengths and needs. Whether we're single or not, we need multiple "Touchstones," people who bring us comfort and help us feel safe and loved. Beyond "Sounding Boards," we need "Frolickers," the people who remind us to have fun, and "Truth Tellers," who help us face the truth, whether we ask them to or not. If there are gaps in your safety net, it's time to fix it. Remember, you don't have to go it alone even when you're single.

Lately, I feel like I'm reaching a new, deeper level of peaceful love and understanding for myself that's hard to explain. I've never been more confident and settled in who I am and where

I'm going. I know that I'm on the right path. I've been surprised to discover that this feeling I have for myself extends to other people in my life too. Realizing a greater love for myself has helped me love others more deeply.

I realized the other day that I'm quite content being on my own now and that it would take someone extraordinary to make me want to change that; Mr. Right rather than Mr. Right Now. I know that if the time is right, the right person will come into my life, but I'm not worried about that. I know I've already found the love of my life – and it's me.

What would your wedding vows be to yourself?

True Beauty

I had the pleasure of seeing one of my favorite speakers, Bonnie Bing, at a Wichita Independent Business Association Women's Leadership Alliance meeting. Bonnie is a journalist and always speaks her truth while being hilariously funny at the same time. Besides that, I just love seeing her.

I've known Bonnie most of my life. She was a teacher and my gym coach during one of the most awkward times in any woman's life – the junior high school years. From the time I was 13 until I was 16, I saw her every school day in gym class. People often ask me what Bonnie was like as a teacher, and I always say, "When a chubby girl still likes her gym coach, that says something." In P. E. class and since, Bonnie has always been kind, patient, encouraging, and supportive of me. She's one of my role models, mentors, and favorite people.

I wonder how many women can say that? I suspect many were terrorized by gym coaches and others, causing them to feel ashamed of their bodies, dealing crushing blows to their self-esteem. In case you didn't realize, body shaming isn't something that happens only to women who are plump. It affects almost all women, shamed for not measuring up to a photo-edited ideal, including being skinny and "too pretty."

So many women struggle with feeling comfortable in their own skin. It makes us avoid cameras and not be present in our lives. This disconnect hit home for me several years ago when a close friend died. I noticed that I wasn't in any of the pictures on the memorial slide show. I know I was at these parties and events but had hidden from the camera. It was as if I didn't exist in this person's life. It made me rethink how the rest of my life will be documented.

One of the most profound insights I've gained from the Finishing School is how I see myself. I owe a lot of that to my former administrative assistant, Jessica Wasson, the woman that helped create the look of the Finishing School brand. In so many ways, this millennial has been influential in my life.

I love my millennial mentor

Even though Jessica is nearly half my age, she's another of my role models, mentors, and favorite people. Because of her, I started making short videos to promote our classes. I told her I hated to see myself on video, and she demanded that I do it anyway. Jessica told me, "People like seeing you in person. So why wouldn't they want to see you in a video?" If her sassy ass hadn't helped me break through that barrier, I never would have had the confidence to teach Finishing School classes online.

Body image is not only the way we see our bodies. It's also about the way we assume other people see us. The problem with these assumptions is that the way we see ourselves is subjective. It's not based on fact. Body image is our perception, imagination, emotions, and physical feelings of and about our bodies. It's in our heads and is much more influenced by our self-esteem than how others judge us. So while we obsess about certain flawed body parts, the world sees us as a whole person, including our spirit's inner glow.

We don't even realize how we're letting this obsession with image steal our power. Social media is compounding the damage of negative body image by projecting perfectionist pressure for us to obsess over. We've been shamed into succumbing to frauds and illusions. It holds us back from showing the world who we truly are. We must learn to question the unrealistic expectations we've let society – and ourselves – put on us. It is completely, crazily, over the top unrealistic to think every woman can, or should, look like a model.

The first person we have to convince to change this way of thinking is ourselves. We need to reframe and refocus how we look at the gallery of our space and take time to celebrate the love we have for ourselves, warts and all.

Self-love is about acceptance and seeing yourself as the gift you are. Today you can choose to love yourself and respect your body. You can listen to it and honor what it needs. You can see your body as a tool and a teammate that helps you live your full potential. You are more beautiful than you realize.

Step outside yourself and ask, "What is the beauty others see in me?"

12 Tips for a Positive Body Image

Choose to look at yourself and your body in a more positive way. The more you practice these thought patterns, the better you'll feel about who you are and the body you naturally have.

1. **Appreciate all that your body can do.**
   Every day your body works to carry you closer to your dreams. Celebrate all of the amazing things your body does for you—running, dancing, breathing, laughing, dreaming, and more.

2. **Keep a top-ten list of things you like about yourself.**
   List things that aren't related to body size or what you look like. Read your list often. Add to it as you discover more things to like about yourself.

3. **Remind yourself that "true beauty" is not simply skin deep.**
   When you feel good about yourself and who you are, you carry yourself with a sense of confidence, self-acceptance, and openness that makes you more beautiful. Beauty is a state of mind, not a state of your body.

4. **Look at yourself as a whole person.**
   Stop being mean to yourself when you see yourself in a mirror or in your mind. Choose not to focus on specific body parts. Instead, see yourself as you want others to see you–as a whole person.

5. **Surround yourself with positive people.**
   It is easier to feel good about yourself and your body when you are around supportive people who recognize the importance of liking yourself just as you naturally are.

6. **Stop letting a look or comment from someone else determine how you feel about yourself.**
   That person probably wasn't judging you, but you are judging yourself. So instead, try saying to yourself, "I forgive you. I send you love."

7. **Don't join in when your friends compare and trash their bodies and talk about dieting.**
   You hurt your self-image when you bash your body in conversations with others. Instead, celebrate your natural beauty and each other's successes.

8. **Shut down those voices in your head that tell you your body is not "right" or that you are a "bad" person.**
   You can overpower those negative thoughts with positive ones. The next time you start to tear yourself down, build yourself back up with a few quick affirmations that work for you. For example, "My body is powerful!"

9. **Work with your body, not against it.**
   Wear comfortable clothes that fit and make you feel good about your body. Then, add some pizzazz and personality

with fun, colorful accessories.

10. **Become a critical viewer of social and media messages.**
Pay attention to images, slogans, or attitudes that make you feel bad about yourself or your body. Then, challenge these messages: write a letter to the advertiser or talk back to the image or message.

11. **Do something nice for yourself.**
Do something that lets your body know you appreciate it. For example, take a bubble bath, make time for a nap, or find a peaceful place outside to relax.

12. **Use the time and energy that you might have spent worrying about food, calories, and weight to do something to help others.**
Sometimes reaching out to other people can help you feel better about yourself and can make a positive change in our world.

What first little step will you take to shine some love on your body image?

No Shame

I've been fat my entire life. The reason I know I'm fat is that people have been telling me so since I was a child. At school, riding my bike down the street, and even at home, people constantly felt compelled to let me know that I was a fatty.

Some comments and name-calling were purposely mean. Others, intending to be helpful and caring, were unknowingly cruel in a more profound way. These "helpful" comments had a profound effect when given by people I loved and trusted.

Today when I look back at pictures of myself as a child, the reality of the situation confuses me. I would hardly call myself "fat" at that time in my life. I wasn't skinny by any means but scarcely worthy of the attention I received.

This little girl was told she was fat

I want to blame Twiggy for my pain. The super skinny model nicknamed for her build became the "Face of 1966" when she was 16 and weighed 112 pounds. This radically changed the ideal body type for everyone, morphing from curvy Marilyn Monroe to stick-straight Twiggy in the blink of an eye.

I went on my first diet when I was in fifth grade. I remember eating lots of cottage cheese, tuna, and melba toast. I'll never forget the school nurse taking me out of class every week to weigh me on the scale in her office to see how many pounds I'd lost. The short walk down the hall back to the classroom was mortifying, knowing everyone was expecting a report of how I'd done. I can still see the linoleum-tiled floor of that hallway in my head.

When I was in my 20s, I read "Fat is a Feminist Issue" by Susie Orbach, and it changed the way I think about being fat. I found a paper I wrote about the book recently while cleaning out my attic, and it reminded me of when my eyes opened to see this issue for what it is.

This book helped me see how fat people are discriminated against and shunned for not fitting into the ideal mold of how women are "supposed" to look. It helped me recognize the hypocritical messages and misinformation we receive around food and see the weight control industry for the scam it is. But, most importantly, it taught me not to be ashamed of my body and to learn to love myself no matter what size.

I got angry. I fantasized about taking down the size exclusive 5-7-9 clothing stores. I got loud about body positivity. I learned more about the weight control industry and got mad that we pay them billions of dollars a year to shame us into losing weight with plans that go against our biology and are destined to fail. (In the United States, we spent $70 billion in 2018, and this amount grows every year.) Brazenly, I started to own my hefty power.

I remember the exact moment I turned it around and stopped being shamed for my size. I had picked my little brother up when he got out of school, and we were sitting in a fast-food parking lot eating and talking. It was the first thing I'd had to eat all day, and I may have been a little "hangry."

A gaggle of skinny, blonde girls got off a school bus on the corner, and while they walked past us, they started making oinking, piggy sounds. I'd had enough. I started my car, revved the engine, and chased them wildly through the neighborhood with a vengeance that scared the daylights out of them and my brother.

Of course, I wouldn't really have run them down, but their screams and terror in their eyes said they didn't know that. Hopefully, they thought twice about doing something like that again. The most intriguing thing about that experience is that people stopped saying those kinds of things to me after that day. Maybe the homicidal gleam in my eye makes them think twice.

I'm still angry. Every time I try to write about this topic, the results are much too fiery. I'm mad about stupid diets I've let myself be pressured into. I'm livid about drinking disgusting grainy liquids that stole the joy from my life and made me feel punished for eating food. I'm angry with cruel people, with the "best intentions," of course, thinking they know what's best for me and my body.

Emcee on the big stage!

I'm angry at the way I'm treated, dismissed, and ignored because my weight is seen as a weakness of my character. As I was getting ready to go on stage for an event I was emceeing, someone I know walked up to me and said, "Hi, big girl." It took everything I had not to throat punch her. In reality, I was angrier about the "girl" than the "big," but still. I guess I know how she categorizes me now.

Not everyone is destined to be skinny, and that's okay. Skinny does not equal healthy. We need to figure out what works for us and the healthiness of our bodies and not get swept up in the latest diet craze. I could nearly be a nutritionist for all I've researched and learned about the diet du jour, only to find out later it wasn't entirely accurate or even that good for me. My goal is to make peace with food and listen to my body.

I had an experience that woke me up to the wisdom of my body. I was in line at the grocery store when I happened to see a ghost from my past out of the corner of my eye. The minute I saw this person, I started shaking uncontrollably. My reaction was disappointing because I thought I had made more progress than letting a sighting affect me that way.

I told this story to a friend that's an expert on PTSD and co-teacher of our class on transitioning past trauma. She told me, "That wasn't your mind, Jill. That was your body's reaction to the situation." At that moment, I recognized how our bodies react with a mind of their own. It was a fight, flight, freeze response from the ancient limbic part of my brain. My body protected me while my brain was still trying to make sense of the situation.

I started thinking about how horrible I am about listening to my body, limping through the pain, and ignoring all the signals it tries to send me to tell me what it needs. Through dieting, I've conditioned myself to ignore hunger pangs so intensely that I have to teach myself to gauge when I'm starting to get hungry rather than waiting to eat until I'm out-of-control famished.

To work on this, I've started asking my body what it wants. Sometimes out loud. When I'm thinking about what I want to eat, I ask my body, "What do you want for lunch?" The answers have been surprising. It isn't always ice cream. Sometimes it's tuna salad with chopped tomatoes and buttered toast points.

Since I've started doing this, I've lost a little weight, but that's not my focus. Instead, I'm making lasting peace with food and my body by loving and trusting myself. Now that I'm learning to own what works for me, I'm finding that the weight loss I've been fighting with no lasting success since I was five is happening naturally.

Because I'm using intuition to care for my body, I started thinking of this as intuitive eating and looked it up online. To my delight, I found a book by a dietitian/therapist and a nutrition therapist called "Intuitive Eating." The authors have taken the ideas I've just started to play with on my own and perfected them over many years to help people create healthy relationships with food, mind, and body. It is life-changing.

I want you to know if you've been riding the diet roller coaster, it is not your fault. You're not failing. "Diets" defy our body's biological fight to survive, and this survival instinct is much stronger than willpower. When we starve our bodies, whether through a diet or famine, metabolism slows, and our body starts craving carbohydrates, its preferred source of quick energy. This reaction explains why we can't lose weight no matter how little we eat and why carb binges happen before we realize we have a cookie in our mouth. Our bodies are protecting us.

I'm just starting to experiment with Intuitive Eating and am halfway through the book. It's going to take a minute to figure out how to let go of the warped dieting habits I've learned and to pay attention to what works for me. I know it won't be easy, but I'm cautiously optimistic that this is what I've been looking for all along.

Please understand. I'm not in this to lose weight. I'll always be thick and proud. I am very comfortable in my skin and confident in my cuteness. As part of my voyage of self-discovery, I'm learning to listen to my inner wisdom and trust myself. Unpacking the baggage of weight and letting go of old ways will strengthen the most important relationship in my life, the one I have with myself.

What differences have you noticed in how you once saw yourself compared to the reality you see today?

Sparkle

I'm in love with the work of photographer and author Ari Seth Cohen. He's the creator of *Advanced Style,* a project devoted "to capturing the sartorial savvy of the senior set." Inspired by stylish seniors with attitude, Ari seeks out older people who embrace a style all their own and photographs them for his blog, books, and documentaries. He features people who "live life to the fullest, age gracefully and continue to grow and challenge themselves." His mission is to show us that we can be stylish, creative, and vital at any age and celebrate life.

I love that Ari captures these gorgeous creatures on film, but who I really love are the people in his photographs. At a time in life when many women feel invisible, these fashionistas let their freak flag fly and dare to express and represent themselves by the way they dress. These adventurous men and women have turned their appearance into an art form. Since I've learned of his work, I've aspired to be just like his subjects when I grow up and just go for it. Show my sparkle.

Women who have a great sense of style always catch my eye. At one of my favorite Indian restaurants, I kept seeing an older woman who always looked stone-cold fabulous. Her hair was always perfectly coiffed, and her outfits were stylish with expressive colors and lots of leopard print. Every time I saw her, she was perfectly put together, with a style of her own. I couldn't help but notice her. We smiled at each other every time, recognizing a kindred spirit. One day, she walked up and introduced herself. We told each other what we'd been thinking, "Love your style!" I found out during the introduction that I'm friends with two of her also stylish daughters, sealing the connection forever.

A fashionista from an early age

I've always loved fashion and style. I worked at a clothing store in the neighborhood shopping center while in high
school. We mainly sold what I thought of as "old lady" clothes.
The women who worked during the day fit that image to me,
wearing gold pointy-toed Elfin slippers when their feet hurt
from standing all day, fighting over customers and commissions. I thought of them as fashion sharks and stayed far out
of their path, watching and learning how they made sales.

It was one of the most formative jobs I've had, and I met
some colorful characters there that I'll never forget. Like the
woman that worked down the hall at a shoe store, who showed
me the gun she carried in her purse while we were in the dressing room. I met a statuesque, dark-haired, exotic yet sophisti-
cated woman with a great sense of style. Even though she was
a bit older than me, we became friends for a short time and
had fascinating conversations about what she'd seen and done
in her life. I'd just finished reading "Breakfast at Tiffany's," and

talking to her felt like I was living in a Capote novel until she flew away, like Holly Golightly, to another adventure.

The most fun part of the job for me was helping women get out of their style rut. I'd help them pick out clothes they would have never picked for themselves as an "experiment" to try something new. I admit, sometimes I added in some pretty silly outfits. But it was mainly to help them see how less ridiculous something else was that would have been out of their comfort zone before the clown suit – and a little bit to see what I could get away with. You've met me.

As women get older, we often feel invisible. We have been led to believe that we should become more timid as we age, to act and dress appropriately for our age. Who made up that rule?

I've been thinking more about how we present ourselves since I watched "Everybody's Talking About Jamie" on Prime Video. This inspiring story about a young man being true to himself and following through on dreams to live life on his terms made me think.

It doesn't matter if you're a young man who wants to wear a dress to prom or an older woman that wants to wear Care Bear tights – who cares! It hurts no one. But holding people back from who they indeed are, or may become, is harmful.

Having to pretend you are someone you are not, lacking the freedom to live authentically, hurts all of us. Shaming people into narrow confines based on preconceived biases keeps the world from that person's brilliance. Imagine what unique gifts people have and aren't allowed to use. What would the world be like if people were allowed to pursue their dreams?

No matter what society thinks, we don't have to hold ourselves back from authentic self-expression. Here's what I'm thinking.

Don't lose your sparkle.

Let age embolden you to adorn yourself with individuality and creativity and stop caring what others think. I want to see you for who you are, not who you think you should be. It's a much happier way to live.

You don't have to ask for permission.

If you want mermaid hair color or to start wearing a bow tie, do it! You may get some looks and comments, but so what? We don't care. You can get away with nearly anything you dare to do.

Curate your look.

If you love it, wear it. I enjoy seeing kids on the street whose moms let them pick their clothes. They're always so fun and imaginative. They draw my eye right away. Maybe it's just me, but these are the kids I want to hang out with. So much fun!

By the time we're of a certain age, we've been curating our collections of what we love for a long time. Find new, fun ways to put together what you already have to create your unique style. You don't have to go crazy. If you don't like to draw attention to yourself, take baby steps and add just a little flair, like an accessory you love.

Be brave.

What may seem risky may not cause as much stir as we think it will. People may not even notice you've changed your style or are wearing a new hat, so keep trying until they do!

Let go of patriarchal ideals of beauty.

Most of us will never embody the body and image of a perfect woman. And that's okay. It doesn't matter what size you are, how many wrinkles you have, or any other ways you don't fit into the cookie-cutter world of what women are "expected" to be. We come in all shapes, sizes, and colors, and trying to be something we aren't is a distraction from more important ways we could be spending our energy.

You look as good as you feel.

Confidence looks good on you, so clothes that make you feel confident and beautiful are always the right choice. I used to buy clothes just because they fit me, but now I like to put the "Hell Yes!" trick into play. If I try something on and it isn't "Hell Yes!" it's "Hell NO." If something doesn't make you feel fabulous when you try it on, chances are it will not get any better at home, so leave it at the store. If you aren't feeling it, that garment is just not your friend and doesn't get to live in your closet.

Throw out the "rules."

What are too many accessories? When should you stop wearing white? Does this make my butt look too big? Who cares! Free yourself from fashion slavery, and wear whatever you want. If it feels good, wear it and show the world who you really are. And really – Is it a matter of life, or death, to add just one more accessory over the line?

Broaden your horizons.

Because sparkle truly comes from within, a big part of staying vital is continuing to learn and grow as we age. That's why one of the slogans for the Finishing School for Modern Women is, "Not because we need finishing, but because we're never finished."

Work to stay relevant by paying attention to what's going on in the world. Try something new. Make friends with people younger than you. Travel to places you've never been before, in your own backyard and beyond, whether you get there in person or through a book.

Do something new.

When the seasons change, it's a perfect time to transition into something different and jump out of a rut. Try on some new and unexpected clothes or jewelry. If you're stuck, there are stores that offer style consultation services to give you advice to help you change your style.

Go to a salon or makeup counter and get a makeup lesson to update what you've been doing. Talk to your stylist, and explore a new haircut or color. Most salons give free consultations and estimates if you don't have a stylist. Tip: Getting your hair styled is a great no-risk way to try on a new stylist. And remember, it's only hair and will grow back.

If you're a fan of makeover shows, like the original "What to Wear," "Queer Eye," or "100% Hotter," you know that a new look can change a life. There are many people whose profession it is to help you look – and feel better. So don't wait to be nominated for one of these shows. You deserve to live your best life right now, no matter how your body has changed over the years.

Remember that we are mentors.

A good friend pointed out to me recently that as we get older, we are automatically mentors for younger women. We talked about the importance of setting an excellent example in all that we do publicly – especially if we're visible in the community. So, let's show these whippersnappers an example of what it means to live authentically, embracing the fullness of who we are.

What will you do to amp up your style and let your freak flag fly?

Finding Your Purpose

Clearing out my upstairs bedroom to convert it from cluttered storage to a guest room felt a lot like an archeological expedition. Sifting through the layers of my life in boxes archived years ago has been quite an adventure. Living in the same house most of my adult life, I still have lots of stuff from my past that would have been tossed if I'd moved around.

I have so many memories in this house, good and not so good. It's been a bittersweet process. I've tried to take my time and experience the memories and emotions that bubble up from looking at what feels like artifacts from past lives.

I've found things I've been missing for years and other surprises I didn't realize I was missing. But, surprisingly, one of the things I'd forgotten held a significant discovery for me.

When I saw a broken board poking up from one of the boxes, memories flooded back. It may seem like a weird thing to save. Yet, the importance of this item wouldn't have been apparent if anyone other than me had found it.

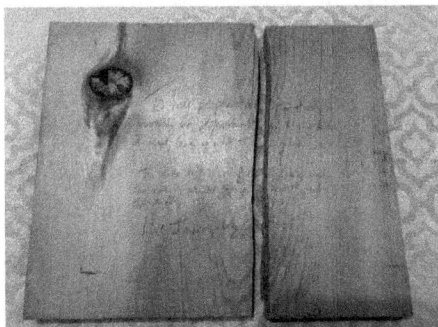

A breakthrough moment

I remember thinking about getting rid of the broken board as I packed it up originally but kept it because of what it symbolized to me. I'm glad I kept it now because it's given me a huge realization about my purpose.

One of my favorite things about working for Aveda for most of my 30s was the excellent training we were given. It changed my life. Salespeople often get sales training from the companies they represent, but the training we got went light years beyond that.

During one training conference, they brought in Kung Fu masters to help us learn to break through what was getting in the way of achieving our goals. We were to each pick a board and write the goal we wanted to accomplish on one side and what was holding us back from that goal on the other side of the board. Then, they showed us how to push through obstacles to break through to what we wanted to achieve, snapping the board in half with our bare hand.

I remember standing in line, nervous about whether I'd fail to break the board on the first try. So many people were in the room that I wanted to think of me as capable. While I watched, I realized that the least amount of hesitation wouldn't get the job done. The trick, we were told, was to imagine passing through to the other side of the board, to the goal, rather than focusing on the obstacle of the board.

Jill, the Aveda lady

The feeling I got when I broke that board with the force of my hand on the first try is something I'll never forget. Breaking it made me feel like I could accomplish anything! The physical reminder of how I felt that day is why I couldn't toss the board out.

It had been so many years since I'd laid eyes on that board I'd forgotten what I'd written. So when I reread it, my jaw dropped. The goal I'd written over 20 years ago said, "To help people grow spiritually, mentally, and professionally, to give back at least some of what I'm given."

What I'd said was much more than a goal. When I looked at what I'd written, I realized that what I'd created that day was my purpose. One that I'm living today. When I dug deeper, I realized this has always been my ambition. Since then, I've been thinking a lot about how to discover our life's calling.

I invite many guest speakers to the Entrepreneurship in the Arts class I teach in the fall at Wichita State University. One of my favorite guests is a professional musician who bravely shares all the glory and challenges of making her living as a rock star.

In May 2019, this badass was in a horrible car crash and was so severely injured the doctors gave her a 5% chance of survival. That she could walk into class not even six months after the accident, talk and answer questions, and inspire students with her honest vulnerability is nothing short of a miracle.

I've done some work with this musician in my consulting practice. I helped her figure out how to make enough money to pay her band to come and back her up during the anti-bullying programs she did for schools. So I know that part of why she makes music is because it helps people.

But talking to Jenny after class, I can see that she has indeed found her purpose. She believes in the healing power of music as she never has before. She shares and spreads that aspiration through the songs she writes and the people she touches with her singing. I think that's why she's still with us today. She has much more to do.

When you know your purpose, it keeps you rooted to the Earth. It can bring you back to life. But how do you know what it is? How can you find it? And most importantly, how do you believe it?

What are you compelled to do?

What is it you do that you have no choice but to do? It's that thing you can't stop doing. Even if you put it down for a while, you're always drawn back to it. Not even the nay-sayers saying "nay" can stop you. I'm talking about positive things that make you feel good long-term, besides chocolate consumption.

Can you feel it?

We know when things are right because we can feel it in our bodies. It feels expansive – like our hearts are grander than our bodies, filled with peaceful, joyous energy. I know something is a good idea when I get a massive case of goosebumps.

What do you feel fearless about?

Taking risks is part of finding your purpose. Trial and error. Fits and starts. Even when taking one step forward results in taking three steps back, these setbacks don't phase you. For very long, anyway. It takes this fearlessness to keep going, to find your way.

How does this help other people?

When I'm consulting with someone to help them start a business, the first thing we talk about is what the company does for its customers. Does it take away their pain? Make their life more worth living? What customer needs will be solved with your product/service?

Of course, your purpose doesn't have to be for the betterment of humankind. After all, we must learn to take care of ourselves too. But why not? Why hide your light? There is so much more to gain by sharing with others and growing together. Vibrating at a higher frequency brings everyone up.

Life is interesting. I can see now that so much of what I've done throughout my life has landed me right where I am today. Exactly where I'm supposed to be. Maybe part of finding our purpose is gradually letting it come to us, following our heart to the next leg of the journey.

What is your purpose?

Let it Shine!

Music inspires me. No matter what mood I'm in, there's a song that fits how I feel – or want to feel. I listen to the "Wonder Woman Theme" song when I want to feel more powerful. When I'm facing adversity, I turn to "Stand" by Sly and the Family Stone. Songs pop into my head all the time. These spontaneous songs often have a hidden message for me that's bubbled up from my brain without even realizing it. I've started paying more attention to this.

The song that gets caught on repeat in my head is "This Little Light of Mine." Since I was a little girl in church, this song has significantly influenced my life. When I was a child, I took the meaning very literally. Even today, when I sing this song in my head, I can feel the light that lives inside my heart. The knowledge that we all have this light of love and brilliance living inside us warms me. When I am in doubt, it reminds me to let my light shine.

Too often, we hide our light. What we all have to offer the world is so amazing, yet we doubt ourselves and let fear keep us from our purpose. I read an article several years ago about self-doubt and how selfish it is not to share our ideas. We think our opinions don't matter and our ideas are stupid. So we keep them to ourselves rather than sharing them with others. Maybe it's not always the next great breakthrough, but our ideas can reach beyond us to inspire others in ways we don't even realize. But not if we don't speak our minds.

Imposter Syndrome, that panicky feeling that we're a fraud, and everyone will find out, is real. It's a trick that our inner critic plays to keep us safe. Whenever we attempt a risk, this

Letting my light shine

voice of inner doubt starts picking at us, giving reasons why we should keep our lips zipped and not take a chance. Sure, this could keep us safe from vulnerabilities, but what good does that do? If we don't take risks, we don't grow.

One of the missions of the Finishing School for Modern Women is to help you shine your light, discover your authentic self and become more the woman you want to be. Life is a challenging journey, and it is much easier made together. Gathering women to talk about our vulnerabilities and issues is powerful, and I am always amazed at the healing energy we create when our inner light unites.

You are worthy of greatness. Show it to the world!

What will you do to let the world see your greatness?

Chapter Two

Never Finish Feeling

How We Treat Our Emotions

1. Working up the Nerve

2. Well, That was Crappy!

3. Overwhelm!

4. Broken Hearted

5. Practicing Patience

6. When Did That Happen?

7. See What You Did?

Working up the Nerve

I spent most of yesterday feeling a bit nervous. I had a short but important presentation to give, so the appointment was on my mind. I may look calm and smooth on the outside, but I'm paddling like hell on the inside!

I don't think there's anything wrong with being a little nervous. It's normal to feel that way when we care about the results. And, if we don't care about the results, why do it?

I never let the nervousness take over like I used to when I was younger. When I hear myself say, "I'm so nervous," over and over again, I know I've got to talk myself in off the ledge! I counter with something like, "You've got this." Or "This is what you do!" It helps because I know it's true.

This topic came up in the Entrepreneurship in the Arts class I teach at Wichita State University. Each semester I invite guest speakers who make a living in the arts industry to help students learn from their experiences. Our guest Monte Wheeler, the new owner of Mosely Street Melodrama, a local theater company, brought up how much courage it takes to put yourself out there. When he was starting and new to auditions in New York City, he told us that he wore the widest leg pants possible, so no one could see his knees shake.

I had many epiphanies during Monte's visit. My favorite was about "building your core," or in other words, the inner strength that helps us take risks. I'd never thought of it like that before, and it makes a lot of sense. We work on our core muscles during exercise classes. So why shouldn't we work on our mental "core" as well?

Through co-teaching classes on transitioning trauma at the Finishing School for Modern Women, I've learned a bit about reconnecting with resilience after trauma. We're all born with the ability to bounce back from whatever life throws at us. The proof – we're already survivors!

We can strengthen our ability to spring back by practicing coping strategies in advance, like building a coping savings account. When we're feeling strong, situations don't kick us in the gut quite as hard as when we're feeling vulnerable.

Before this conversation, I'd thought of these pre-emptive coping strategies more as "self-care." Now, thanks to Monte, I see that it's so much more than that. It's about building confidence.

Purposely working to develop our self-esteem like a muscle is powerful. Talk about "building the core!" I reached out on social media and asked, "What do you do to build confidence?" So many fantastic suggestions flowed in, so I used a few of these ideas to build myself up before the presentation. Here are my favorites.

When you look good, you feel good.

If we were playing Family Feud, "upping your appearance game" would be the number one answer to my question about building confidence. Lots of people told me that sprucing up their outer appearance helped their inner mood. For example, simply putting on a bold lip color raised confidence levels for many women who responded. I know screaming red lipstick does it for me.

Dressing up, going bold with color, or wearing power accessories were brought up many times too. One person said that wearing jewelry gifted to her by another powerful woman made her feel more confident, visualizing the bracelet as a repository of her friend's energy.

One delightfully surprising answer was about feeling comfortable in our own skins. A woman in an online intuitive eating group I follow said that walking around her house naked makes her feel more confident. She said her husband doesn't hate it either. I couldn't love this more.

It doesn't take binge-watching too many makeover shows to know how this works. There are actually good reasons to get that new haircut and color, buy a new fancy frock or a pair of statement shoes.

Bow to the Queen!

You are what you think.

Just like you are what you eat, you are what you think. The number two answer to building confidence was paying attention to what we tell ourselves. Some people start their day with power affirmations, like "I am..." statements. My favorite example was, "I am courageous, and I stand up for myself."

Other people talked about gratitude – acknowledging the blessings in their lives, the good things that have happened with more to come, and being thankful that things are getting better every day. One answer along this vein that surprised me was an act of giving back by doing something kind for someone else. That's gratitude in action.

I like mantras, phrases I tell myself to help get my head back on straight. For example, after presentations, my usual habit is to replay everything in my head and pick it apart, which, of course, does no good. To change this miserable habit, I've learned to stop the replay and repeated something my Dad told me after an incredibly hard day, "All you can do is the best you can do, and that's all you can do." Then I let it go.

You can do it!

Another frequent answer to build confidence was to get moving and making. Popular answers were exercising, walking in nature, and having a personal dance party. Thinking about movement as something that feels good is more fun than thinking you have to "work out" to exercise. For example, I love yoga for my poor arthritic joints. It makes me more confident when I can move with more fluidity from a half-hour of gentle stretches.

Just listening to music helps too. How can you help but shake your bootie or chair dance, at least a little, to some pumping tunes? Artists like Cardi B, Fergie, and Latin music were some of the top music jams mentioned. I love Lizzo so much. You can dance and repeat power affirmations simultaneously with her music.

Getting creative and making whatever strikes your fancy builds confidence too. Whether art-related, craft-inspired, or culinarily created, it feels good to use our imagination to make beautiful things come from our hands. Home improvement projects count too. Nothing builds confidence like seeing the results of your handiwork in whatever genre inspires you.

You are loved.

This popular theme surprised me the most. Having the love and support of the people in our lives apparently goes a long way toward building confidence. Knowing that someone we revere sees what is good enough in us to love helps us understand these values in the reflection.

But the most surprising answer in this category were those that had to do with the people who came before us and the strength we've gained from their struggles. A friend had this to say: "I think about my ancestors behind me – loving me, rooting for me. However lacking and weak I'm feeling, generations of people came before me who had many fewer choices, and many of them died too soon. And thinking about that, I can do my best. I am big and strong with their hope."

You are love.

I've always thought the way we protect our vulnerability is to "grow a rhino suit," a thick skin that repels the slings and arrows of life so no one can get through. But, one of the biggest epiphanies I had in class with Monte was the realization that building our core is a whole other way of protecting ourselves.

Building our core and working on self-confidence really boils down to our ability to give ourselves unconditional love, not just protect ourselves. Looking at caring for ourselves in this way is so much more expansive. It grows our hearts rather than throwing up a shield.

We agreed in class that life takes both a strong core and a rugged rhino suit. The trick is to know which one to use and how and when to employ them. I have a feeling that strengthening the core is where the big paybacks happen.

What do you do to build confidence?

Well, That was Crappy!

Raise your hand if you've had a crappy week.

That's what I thought. So many hands!

I don't know what's in the air, but this past week seems to have been hard on lots of people, including me. Maybe it's the full moon this weekend that's fueling this rough cycle, or perhaps it's the end of the school year and everything that goes with it stressing everyone out.

Reading my friends' Facebook posts, I wondered if the feed was being manipulated to see how people would react to so much unpleasant news. There have been friends with loved ones moving on to become one with the universe, precious furry friends scampering over the rainbow bridge, and a gamut of other soul-crushing news. So when I read that Millie the Weather Dog, who's been charming us on a local news channel for 14 years, had passed, I cried.

Putting on big events is BIG stress

I've had my own stressors to deal with this week too. Co-chairing the last year of a massive fundraiser for the Friends of the Wichita Art Museum with a 60-year tradition was much more stressful than I thought it would be. So many people were disappointed to see the event come to an end and let me know in no uncertain terms. All the emotions like guilt, sadness, shame, and mourning loss tripped my triggers and have been a lot to process.

At a very well-timed prescheduled appointment with my therapist, she gave me incredible insights. She asked me what I was doing to cope with the stress in my life. I gave a few lame answers about self-care. That wasn't what she was looking for. In our conversation, I realized that I had utterly abandoned my go-to coping skills. She told me, "That's how you know it is trauma you're dealing with, rather than stress." BOOM! Mind blown.

There's a lot of suffering in the world. In a conversation recently, my mom said that she couldn't imagine that anyone could make it well into adulthood without experiencing some kind of trauma. Yet, although we all have varying degrees of it in our lives, it's one of those things we don't talk about.

And in talking about it, I don't mean rehashing the past. I mean having conversations about how we can transcend it and keep moving forward. Our trauma doesn't define us. It gives us new strengths and makes us who we are. We need to talk about our experiences because no one can work through them on their own.

Sometimes to get to the goal line of a big project, we make ourselves rush from one task to another to hit the deadline while ignoring everything else that comes up along the way. If we think about any of it too much or peek at the audacity of what we're trying to pull off, it becomes completely overwhelming and stupefying.

One of my dearest friends, who has the enormous job of pulling off all the marketing for the biggest public events in Wichita in a one-woman department, calls this, "Chop wood.

Carry Water." We keep moving, no matter the personal costs –
physically, emotionally, and spiritually. Another woman I love
and respect for the selfless work she does in the community
spent the week grounded in bed after pushing her body near
the breaking point.

While our work is important, we have to ask ourselves, is it
truly worth the sacrifice? Especially since no good deed goes
unpunished. That is the big, uncomfortable question. But, on
the other hand, sometimes the next big question has to be, "If
I don't make this happen, who will?"

For change to happen, it takes a fearless visionary to help
focus the people's energy who want to accomplish the same
goals. It's not an easy job, and not everyone can do it. But
when you do have that capability, is it your responsibility to
stick your neck out?

Because you can do it, having refined the skills and reputation to lead, should you do it? In some ways, I do think it is our
responsibility. I've always believed we're each on this planet to
make it a better place to live for everyone, not just ourselves.
I'm trying to find a reasonable balance to this, and if you figure
it out first, please clue me in.

So, I decided I needed a list of my coping skills to revisit
when I feel at the end of my rope. I asked for help from our
network of Modern Women and have added in some of their
suggestions too. Modern Women are so smart!

Take some time for yourself.

I ended up playing hooky on a workday, giving myself permission to take the day off and spend time at home with the
poodle. I spent most of the day being depressed and taking
naps but taking one day off for a mental health pity party and
rest is perfectly reasonable.

My friend Jeanne said, "I try to allow myself time to enjoy
something without judging myself about it being too shallow,

trivial, or a waste of time. I create something like cookies, a garment, or a pretty view. I try to balance accomplishing needed tasks with wanted ones and make a physical note of it to see it adding up and 'counting.' I remind myself that what I can do around here is valued and appreciated, even if not perfectly done. I repeat to myself that I am loved and valued for who I am, not just for what I can do, and I keep saying it even if I can't quite believe it myself at that moment."

Get outside.

Jack and I went to the dog park. It was a beautiful day for it. Getting outside and feeling the sun on my skin felt good. I'd forgotten how stress relieving it is to be at the park, laughing at the crazy dog antics and letting everything else go.

Advice from Heather: "I like to go camping. Or even a day at the lake with limited phone time to take pictures only. Riding my bike goes to the top of the list. It is easy, and I can do it with minimal fuss."

Get some sleep.

By Tuesday night, I figured out that I needed more sleep and went to bed early. I should have known it since I wanted to throw a tantrum like a petulant toddler. I felt a world better on Wednesday.

Lezlee says she loves a good nap when she's feeling sluggish.

Use your tools.

I always forget about, or maybe just don't take time for, tools that I know help me – like aromatherapy. I worked with Aveda for eight years and became a certified Aromaologist, which combines aromatherapy with wellness practices.

Coupling the aromas of essential oils with activities like breathing exercises, yoga, or meditation takes these practices to the next level. It also conditions the brain over time to get back into a relaxed state just by smelling that same aroma again, thanks to how our brain processes memory.

Nancy says: "Never underestimate the power of "Let It Whip" by The Daz Band. My go-to for unfunking my mood with funk. Also, I cannot ever NOT smile while jumping on the mini-trampoline I got for free from my neighbor's trash. AND apparently, it works miracles on your lymphatic system. Jumping WHILE LISTENING TO "LET IT WHIP?" Off the charts happiness."

Practice saying no.

Now that I've passed the gavel of my board chair position on to the next person who can't say "no," and the event I've co-chaired for several years is no more, it would be easy to start looking around right away for something new. But instead, I've decided to take a bit of time for myself. I need to spend my focus and brainpower on my own priorities before taking on anything new.

Connect.

Great insight from Amy: "What keeps me going is the relationship I have with myself, my integrity, my ongoing development as a human, doing what's right even when others are not, taking a stand for myself and others in the face of adversarial life situations. It's the web of connection we all have with one another, making eye contact and communicating (without words). I am here, and I am with you."

Marilyn suggested, "Spend quality time with the people you love."

Seek out beauty.

I love this suggestion from Lisa: "The way I care for myself in times of stress is by taking my camera and going out to search for beauty. When I'm out in nature, I stop focusing on the daily struggles and instead use the camera as my eyes. Through the camera lens, I notice tiny, beautiful things that I otherwise would miss. It's a reminder that I'm one small part of a much bigger and miraculous world. Perspective is everything."

Reflect.

Every time I start to feel like the world is crashing in, it's usually because I haven't taken the time to develop a plan. It takes a minute to regroup after wrapping up a big project, and there needs to be a mourning period to debrief after the end of something big.

Now is the perfect time to ask yourself questions like, "Is being an overachiever a way to avoid working on what I don't want to but need to do?" I'm going to set some new boundaries in my plan too, so I have something left for me at the end of the day.

While this week started out crappy, it's ended on a high note. Things usually work out that way. Keeping these coping strategies close at hand will be a good reminder the next time I'm feeling super stressed. Enjoy your life!

What coping skills will you practice when you get super stressed?

OVERWHELM!

Usually, it isn't until I start explaining what I "do" when I meet someone new that I begin to feel overwhelmed. As I'm talking about all the professional endeavors and volunteer services I'm working on, even I start to wonder just how much one person can do.

I used to start my professional bio with the phrase, "Jill D. Miller is a World Champion Plate Spinner." I'm amused by the visual description of trying to keep all my plates or responsibilities spinning on the top of long, slender poles as I deftly prance from one "plate" to another, giving it just the right twist to stay aloft. However, I quit using it when people expected me to literally spin plates at speaking engagements.

Fortunately, I love what I'm involved in, or I wouldn't do it. About ten years ago, I adopted a "Joy Suck Rule." I decided if something is sucking the joy out of my life, it has to go! This rule hasn't always been easy to follow, and I don't make the decision lightly. I explore many angles before I decide to cut someone or something out of my life. But in the end, I always know the right thing to do if I'm really listening to myself.

I also know I start new projects to avoid listening to myself. It's a great excuse to be "too busy" to deal with whatever it is I'm trying to avoid. Or at least that's the story I'm telling myself.

Around the time of the big Women's Fair Expo, I hit the wall. Everything caught up with me, and I had a full-blown-overwhelm-panic-attack-melt-down. Now, I'm not telling you this for sympathy. I'm writing about this for a few reasons.

Sometimes people get put into boxes with the expectation that they always act in specific ways, like being happy all the time. So, when the person has a bad day or doesn't have a 100% positive attitude, it disrupts the worldview of the people who boxed them in.

Recently I told a woman about "being in a dark place." She told me she couldn't imagine me ever shedding a tear. I assured her that although I can't ugly cry for some reason, I certainly shed tears. Everyone does. I'm human, just like everyone else. We all struggle with our stuff and need to 'fess up to that.

One of the reasons I started the Finishing School is to get better together. Writing about things, especially for my Modern Women, helps me process what I'm thinking to share with you. I also hope that what I write will help others going through the same things and give you something to think about.

Approaching the tiptop of the big drop

On a particularly bad day, smack dab in the middle of OVERWHELM and on the verge of exhaustion, I opened up to a good friend and told her how I was feeling. We brainstormed ideas. But the best advice she gave me was that I needed to do something about what I was feeling because she'd noticed that I had been ascending a big, overwhelming roller coaster hill – for a while.

So I went home that night, did a lot of soul searching, and started putting together a plan. Now that I'm taking action, rather than feeling powerlessly overwhelmed, I'm feeling more relaxed and better able to hear my inner wisdom that always leads me in the right direction. Best of all, things seem to be magically falling into place since I stopped trying to force things into place. Here's what I've learned.

Ask for help.

I drilled down to figure out that exhaustion was causing me the most problems. I know working long days without any time off isn't good, but sometimes it seems like that's what it takes to get done everything I want to do. I don't like it when the plates crash to the ground. But I also know that keeping up that kind of pace will eventually take a toll on my mind and body.

So, I put together an "Operation: Get Help!" plan. I made a list of specific solutions to explore, people to talk to for advice, and things I could do right away to make my life easier. I asked myself some hard questions about the stories I've been telling myself. Then, I looked at the false benefits these stories gave me to change my narrative and stop what isn't serving me.

Get some advice.

I learned, at a recent conference, "You are only limited by what you know. Ask those around you what they know." At a different conference I went to the following week, I discovered the importance of having a group of people that I can trust that will tell me the truth, no matter what. This insight helped me put together what I call my "Worthy Woman's Club" to help me see things more clearly.

These busy women I admire recently met at my office to give me advice. I was candid and open about what I was doing and thinking, and while it was super vulnerable and uncomfortable for me, I learned a lot. One of the best pieces of advice they gave me was, "slow your roll." I am a harsh taskmaster when it comes to the deadlines and goals I set for myself, and they assured me I wouldn't let anyone down if it took me longer to achieve them.

I had other incredibly impactful one-on-one conversations with other advisers. They helped me make easy decisions over issues I'd been grappling over and gave me more significant insights into who I am and what I'm doing. Most importantly, they helped reinforce that I am on the right path.

Get some help.

Asking for help is something I'm working on, and it feels like such a vulnerable thing to do. Still, I realize I can't do everything myself, so I put together a list of things I can get help for and have started asking for volunteers. Some of the asks have been awesome; others have not. Of course, the ones that didn't pan out so well were unexpected and stung a little. One of the downsides of being transparent is it can bite you in the butt sometimes. Still, I'd rather know those truths sooner than later, about who can be trusted and who will come through when needed.

Read about it.

I love to read, and occasionally I'll slip a personal growth book in the mix. I've had so many Modern Women tell me they're reading "*You are a Badass: How to Stop Doubting Your Greatness and Start Living an Awesome Life*" by Jen Sincero that I had to pick it up. I highly recommend this book! I like to read about what other people have learned in their struggle for greatness, and this book does not disappoint! It's so good; I've reread some chapters several times. It has helped me a lot.

Fan bliss with Jen Sincero

While self-help books give lots of insights, I believe there is a lot to learn from "made up" stories too. Fairytales, myths, and other fictional works are filled with cautionary tales and lessons learned. The important thing is to find what you enjoy and keep reading.

Have a plan.

Putting together my plan of action was one of the best things I did. Maybe it's just the overachiever in me, but I always feel better when I face the situation head-on and decide what to do about it. It makes me feel less helpless when I realize I can change what I don't like. I am fully in charge of my life and happiness. I may not do everything on the list, and it may not work out as I'd intended, but just writing it out gives me direction and starts the energy flowing again.

Surrender.

The biggest lesson I've learned from being in over my head is the importance of the word I set as my theme for 2018:

Surrender. This word doesn't mean "give up" to me. I'm far too stubborn for that! Rather, for me, it means letting go of control; releasing my death-like grip on agendas; having faith that help will come when I need it; and letting go of fear. One of my dear Worthy Women gave me a new mantra for this, "There is no faith where there is fear."

I've been meditating on this idea and asking for peace, and it is working. It's such a relief to let go of the things I can't control. And since I really can't control anything besides my reactions, I can choose to react with faith. It's interesting how much clearer things have become.

Love Yourself.

Spoiler alert: this is a recurring theme in Jen's Badass book. My favorite quote is from Chapter 12. "Love yourself, and the bluebirds of happiness will be your permanent backup singers."

What actions will you take the next time you're feeling overwhelmed?

Broken Hearted

Looking to the future

Isn't it funny what you remember from a picture and what others see when they look at it? Recently, I posted this picture of myself from 1989 on social media after many of my friends posted their headshots of yore.

As my friends were telling me how beautiful the photo was, using words like angelic and ethereal, all I could think of was how incredibly heartbroken I was at the time. I can still see it in my eyes and restrained, down-turned smile. I can remember the feelings of aching despair, ever-present pain and loneliness, and the fear that I would never love again after a failed marriage.

This picture represents something more to me than a headshot. It was part of my reinvention. It was something I did for myself, to help me feel alive and beautiful again, to lift myself out of the depths of divorce hell, a phoenix rising from the ashes.

At the time, I was manager of the Hair Force, the most fabulous salon in all of Wichita during the '80s. We did fashion shows and photoshoots all the time, just for fun, so I asked my friends for help. My friend Tod, who now co-owns the salon Planet Hair, did my makeup and hair to seem swept by the wind.

Linda, Tod's wife and business partner, helped me put together my outfit with a white sheet, photo clamps, and yards and yards of pink tulle. I love those two dearly and still regard them as my closest friends. My long-time friend, Mike Fizer, who has gone on to be an award-winning aviation photographer, did a fantastic job capturing the mood I wanted, of looking hopefully toward the future. The drama of it all makes me chuckle a little today.

When I look back, I seem so young then. It wasn't my first heartbreak, but it was definitely the first really big one. I felt like my legs had been knocked out from underneath me, completely taken by surprise. My life turned upside down when my husband had an affair and left me for a hussy. The buckets of tears I cried!

I'm sure I wore a lot of people out, talking endlessly about my sorrow, trying to understand the unfairness of it all. I am eternally grateful for my mother, who is always there for me – patient, kind, and reassuring, giving great advice and comfort. She's not timid about kicking me in the butt when I need it and is a truth-teller. I know how lucky that makes me.

If I could go back and give that young woman advice, I know what I would tell her. If you're heartbroken, no matter the circumstances, I hope these tips will help you.

Be easy with yourself.

Change takes time. Lick your wounds. Take good care of yourself. Slow down and be careful, as we are more prone to accidents during times of heartbreak. It takes energy and a lot of our attention to experience these emotions.

It's okay to feel sad.

When things change and come to an end, we need to mourn. That includes sorting out the feelings that come with this. Writing about what I'm feeling helps me. For some people, other creative activities, like making artwork or music, help them experience their emotions. For others, physical activity, like dancing or running, gives them the headspace to think. Find what works best for you, and make friends with the pain.

Avoid the drama.

We lash out when we're hurt, hoping it will make us feel better. It doesn't. Even when you feel self-righteously justified, remember that things will look different when you're not in the passion of the moment. Bringing in the theatrics makes you look bad, not them, no matter how right you are. So if you're about to go full-blown drama queen – just step away. A true Queen earns her crown by holding her head high in the air.

Recognize the difference between loneliness and longing.

Longing is loneliness's evil twin. When we get lonely, we start longing for what we don't have. Sometimes we romanticize what we lost into something it never was or think it will never come again. That ravenous desire to end loneliness causes people to make unfortunate choices and take risks that don't serve them.

Spending this energy connecting to yourself to heal and work on a loving relationship with you is what truly cures longing. Listening to love songs and pretending they were from me to me was oddly helpful. When was the last time you told yourself, "I love you?"

Reach out to friends.

I don't think I could have made it through my life without the love of my friends. They've seen me through so many highs and lows. I've learned who I can count on when I need help. I've also learned who I can't count on, which always comes as a disappointment.

I've learned that certain friends are best at specific things and to go to that specialist for what ails me. I know who my truth-tellers are, and I value and listen to them.

Depression is such a liar; I don't need people to tell me what they think I want to hear. I want the truth. I also know who to go to if I need a different perspective for another kind of truth. I know who to go to when I just need comfort, someone to listen to, or a shoulder to cry on. And then there are the friends who are just fun to blow off steam with and have some good times. You don't have to be lonely.

Make new friends.

One of the easiest ways to reinvent yourself is to make new friends. Get out there and meet new people. The world is generally a friendly place, and it isn't hard to start up conversations with strangers. Take a risk. I made a friend a long time ago that I sat next to during jury duty. We're still friends today. I watch for the feeling, like magnets coming together, to help me choose who I want to get to know better. I used to think that was rare, but I'm not so sure now.

You will survive.

Gloria Gaynor is right – you will survive. You're a survivor, not a victim, and can make it through whatever life throws at you. You will live to love another day.

A mantra that helps me at times of significant change is, "Stay positive. Focus on the present. Keep moving forward."

This grounds me and helps me pay attention to the important stuff. Letting go of what we can't control, and trusting ourselves to whatever happens in the future, is more powerful than we realize. It's not easy to do, but I promise it gets easier with practice.

Living well is the best revenge.

Since you are the only person you can control, why not go out there and make the best life for yourself that you possibly can. Instead of worrying about what someone else is doing, put that energy into reinventing yourself. What have you always wanted to do? Who do you want to be? When you're at a crossroads in life, you can go anywhere! Which path will you choose? What greatness will you achieve? When the shock wears off a bit, it's possible to get excited about what the next chapter in your life will hold.

What I learned from that heartbreak has helped me bounce back from other challenging times. It's helped me be stronger and wiser, and I really wouldn't change much if I had the chance for do-overs. It's made me who I am today, and I love that!

You will survive!

What advice would you give your younger self?

Practicing Patience

Things don't always work out the way we want. Some days it feels like one step forward is three steps back. People will disappoint us. There will be meltdowns. Big, unexpected expenses will come up. We will want things to happen sooner than they do. But, unfortunately, life doesn't always happen according to our plan.

So, what can we do when life gives us lemons? Practice patience. That's right! (Not the answer you were expecting?) I first learned of this concept while working in sales with Aveda. I was driving around Minneapolis with one of my mentors. We were running late, traffic was slow, and I was getting tense. He told me that many situations in life are meant to allow us to "practice patience." This concept was a big "aha" for me. Working in a job that requires a lot of driving can be dangerous and aggravating. But, learning to practice patience behind the wheel is probably one of the reasons I never had a wreck in my eight years as a road warrior.

Much of life is not within our control. We get frustrated, angry, and upset when we face delays, difficulties, and annoyances causing more distress. Being impatient increases stress hormones and blood pressure, ruins relationships, can cause poor choices, and much more. Taking things personally doesn't help either. When someone doesn't return a call, it may not have anything to do with you. There may be a million reasons why someone couldn't fit that into their day.

When things don't go our way, for example, getting stuck in the slowest line in the grocery, we think of the cause of our impatience as being external – what's going on "out there." Our impatience gets even worse when people, or the situation, aren't meeting our expectations.

The challenge is that our expectations are often out of sync with reality. For example, I've seen many people lose their minds at airport ticket counters when their flight is canceled. No amount of yelling at the gate agent will make that plane take off.

The actual cause of our impatience is what's going on in our minds – it is our response to the situation, not the situation itself. Of course, the only thing we can truly control is how we respond to situations. Granted, this is easier to talk about than to do. It will take practice to let things happen in their own time. Lots of practice. Here are some ideas about how to cultivate more patience in your life.

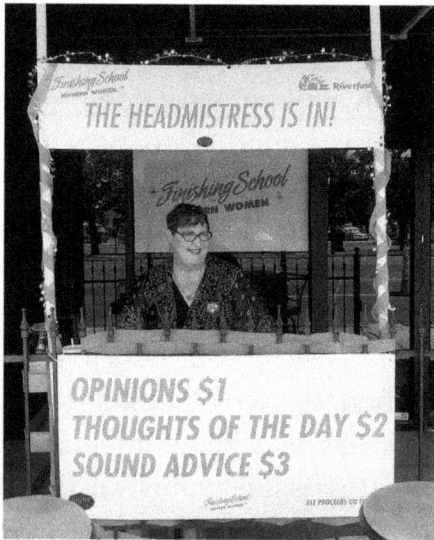

Ask the Headmistress

Breathe!

When we get stressed, our breathing gets shallow. I think of this as breathing from the top part of the lung rather than the deep breaths that come from the diaphragm. Shallow breathing causes less oxygen to make it to the brain, which triggers the flight, fight, or freeze response.

Our body's response to this stress and lack of oxygen increases our heart rate and blood pressure and tenses up muscles to prepare for action. So now we're all revved up and ready to respond in a big way, even when the situation isn't worth getting worked up over.

Amazingly, we can deescalate these responses before inciting a volcanic eruption simply by being conscious of how we're breathing. Oxygen increases by slowing down and taking deeper breaths, which tells our nervous system it's okay to calm down. Pause to breathe.

Once I started paying attention to this, I was surprised at how often I found myself taking shallow breaths or holding my breath. I especially noticed this response in traffic. No wonder I felt stressed out! Now every time I notice I'm breathing through the top part of my lungs, I focus on breathing through my diaphragm. By staying connected to my body in this way, I hope to make deep breaths a habit and keep stress at bay.

Know what triggers you.

You've probably lost your patience enough times in your life that you know what triggers you. Whether it's an irritating coworker or a spouse that doesn't listen, pay attention to what stresses you out and causes you to lose patience.

Once we identify what makes us lose our minds, we can use this information to practice patience. Sometimes simply naming what triggers us takes away some of the power of the response. This awareness can also help us use creative problem-solving skills to figure out ways to avoid situations that set us on fire. For example, making sure your beloved is ready for a conversation before launching into a lecture.

Let it go!

Getting worked up about what we can't control ruins a good mood – and not just for you. Watching videos of "Karens" taking out their frustration on everyone around them is not a good look, although it is amusing when they get hit with instant karma. Don't be that person.

There are so many other things to take up your brain band-width besides what you're irritated about. Switch the channel to something more productive, like what you'll have for dinner tonight or your to-do list. Or more entertaining thoughts like singing your favorite song in your head. Maybe flip to loving thoughts, like how you'll spend time with someone you love. Instead of ruminating about the situation, focusing on loving thoughts will change reactions and make life so much easier – for everyone.

Practice, not perfection.

Remember, being more patient isn't going to happen over-night. It's not a switch you can flip. Start small and try not to get obsessed. Start with minor annoyances one by one and use what you learn about yourself to go after the ones that make the top of your head pop off. Gradually you'll realize there's less to get worked up about than before.

I promise the hard work is worth it. You'll be happier and much more relaxed. Practicing patience allows us to act with grace in situations where we'd typically lose our temper. This inner strength gives us genuine power and lasting progress and makes us more fun to be around.

Happy practicing!

What clues does your body give you to warn you when are getting close to the end of your rope?

When Did That Happen?

I remember the exact moment I realized I was an adult. I was in my early 20s, attending the grand opening of a children's museum in downtown Wichita. One part of the museum was divided into various scenarios, like a restaurant and a broadcast studio. A little girl with long brown hair, probably around 7 years old, was pretending to be a chef in the restaurant kitchen. As I walked into the room, the child started barking orders at me, bossing me around like I was her sous chef. At that exact second, I had the epiphany – "Hey, I'm an adult. I don't have to do anything she says." And I turned around and left the room.

Aging happens so fast. One day you're a fresh-faced adult, starting your life, figuring out who you are and what you want to do, and imagining what the future will hold. The next thing you know – you've hit middle age.

I can remember that moment vividly too. I talked with my cousin when she off-handedly mentioned we had moved into our middle years. I was instantly taken aback. "What? I'm only 44!" I told her. She told me, "How long do you think you're going to live?" Oops! She was right. With female life expectancy at 82 years of age, I guess I'd hit middle age a few years back. (My apologies to those reading this who haven't had that realization yet.)

I should have recognized the hints along the way to help me realize what was going on. Especially as I started getting what I like to call "ma'amed." That's when people in stores and service industries stop calling you "miss" and start calling you "ma'am." In a way, it's a bit disturbing. I remember when my assistant, Jessica, came to work incredulous that she'd just been "ma'amed" for the first time. Suddenly, we'd rather be called "sweetheart" or "honey" instead of the "M" word. I know it's meant as a sign of respect, but it's also an indicator that things are changing, and no matter how young we feel on the inside, the tides of time are moving on.

Now, in my mid-50s, I'm starting to wonder what the indicators of entering the "old-age" stage of life might be. In other words that I don't want to say out loud - how do you know when you're old? Is it when you start getting letters from AARP? Or maybe when you start qualifying for senior discounts? Or maybe, it's when you finally throw away your dusty, outdated, old-lady tampons, at last coming to grips with the fact that you'll never need them again.

I remember feeling
young and
invincible

I am at a stage in life when I go to more funerals than weddings. As the people that take care of me retire, I have to replace the trusted partners I've done business with for a long time, like doctors and home repair people. It seems this life stage I'm dreading is looming ever closer.

I must confess. It gives me a funny, tickly, uncomfortable feeling in my stomach to even type these words. Although I've been thinking about it a lot lately, aging isn't something I want to face. So, I ask myself, "Why is there so much emotion in what is simply life's progression? Why is it such a weird feeling to age? Why do I even care?"

I know in my own relationships, I'm not concerned with how old someone is and have friends of all ages. Which makes me ask myself, "If I don't judge other people for their age, why am I doing this to myself?" Hmm.

Of course, I know what really bothers me is society's perception of aging and the judgments that go along with that. There's such a stigma to getting older we'll go to nearly any lengths to keep the signs of aging at bay.

Some women feel that they disappear as they get older. Others are made to feel irrelevant in the workplace. Ageism is alive and kicking, and discrimination can be subtle yet deadly. No wonder we don't like to admit our age.

I've decided that rather than worry about getting older, I'll focus on maintaining a fresh attitude, something I can control. It may not be the fountain of youth, but I plan to fake it until I make it. Here's my plan.

Not be defined by others' labels.

Have you seen Advanced Style? Created by author and photographer Ari Seth Cohen, this project is devoted "to capturing the sartorial savvy of the senior set." He says, "I feature people who live full creative lives. They live life to the fullest, age gracefully, and continue to grow and challenge themselves." These stylish seniors dress and live for their own amusement and don't care how others think they should behave. While I don't feel I'm quite old enough to join this lively party yet, I aspire to and will start practicing now.

Keep moving.

The best way to stay vital in body, mind, and spirit is to remain mobile. Find whatever this means for you. I already have painful arthritis in my knee and ankles, so walking or running for much distance is not for me. I've found water exercise classes, especially water Tabata, high-intensity interval train-ing, is my jam. I can't even tell I'm sweating. Beyond going to the gym, keeping an active lifestyle with lots of movement of any kind helps too.

Stay involved.

One of the hardest parts about being older is becoming isolated. As friends move on – to become one with the uni-verse or to other locales – we start to lose touch with the physical connections in the community. It's depressing to be by yourself all the time, even with social media. I love how we come together at the Finishing School for Modern Women.

The connections we make in person, and the energy and knowledge we exchange when we're together physically are powerful and feel good. Getting out and volunteering, attend-ing events in the community, and staying engaged are essential to our longevity and connectiveness.

Stay current.

But not with everything. Figure out what makes your heart sing and pursue that. For some, it may be technology, others fashion, music, or current affairs. When I notice that I'm feel-ing left behind because I don't know who some musician, song, or contemporary pop culture craze is, I look it up! It's never been easier to get the information we're curious about with the internet at the tip of our fingers.

But talking to real live people about what they're interested in currently is a great way to keep up too. I've found I learn just as much, if not more, from young people than they can learn from me. Volunteering with young people is a great, no-pressure way to hang out with them. If you don't want a long-term commitment, there are many one-time opportunities to volunteer.

Focus on the fantastic parts of aging.

Sure, everything hurts more, and the stamina I've always depended on doesn't always come through, no matter how hard I try to press on. But, there are lots of good things about being older too.

I'm finally starting to learn how to pick my battles. I've learned a few things and don't have to make the same mistakes I've made in the past. I feel comfortable in my skin and have learned to love myself – not despite my flaws but because of them. I feel much wiser now, making decisions that best serve me, not some idea of what I "should" be, genuinely understanding that I am perfect in my imperfection.

Doing a little research about how you know when you're old, I found that the U.S. Census quantifies middle age as 45 to 65, so I have a way to go before I'm officially "old." Still, I know I'll feel ageless in my head forever. After all, goddesses never age.

What will you do to keep your attitude fresh?

See What You Did!

We have such a tendency to be hard on ourselves, but don't beat yourself up about that. A big part of why this happens is because of the way our brains are hardwired.

We are born with a preprogrammed "negativity bias," which means our brains react stronger and become more active to situations we perceive as negative. This explains why bad news influences our attitudes more than good and why reality and news commentary shows are so popular. We naturally tend to focus on how we failed or didn't quite hit it out of the park rather than what went right.

Of course, it's a good idea to evaluate our experiences, learn how to make things better, and strive for more, but at what point are we successful? Striving for excellence is good, but never being satisfied is miserable. When we constantly ask, "Are we there yet?" it means we're missing out on the sights and experiences along the way. Unfortunately, there is no "there" or magical point in time when we finally feel satisfied. There will always be unfulfilled dreams, especially for big dreamers.

So, what can we do to lighten up? We can celebrate! When a goal is achieved – or even a task – no matter how large or small, take a moment to honor that success. There are so many fantastic reasons to celebrate! It increases our confidence, keeps us motivated, creates a success mindset, and it's just plain fun.

Celebrating doesn't have to be an extravaganza every time. It can be very simple. You can match the celebration to the size of the accomplishment, or you can go big every time.

Celebrating award-winning blogs

My favorite way to reward myself is the gift of time. I love an hour to just do nothing, go to the dog park or soak in the tub. I've always thought it would be fun to start a charm bracelet, buying a new charm for each major accomplishment.

There are so many ways to celebrate yourself. Pick your favorite thing to do and give yourself permission to do your favorite thing guilt-free. You can write a bunch of simple ideas on slips and paper, put them in a jar, and draw one out to celebrate without having to think about it.

Celebrate failures too. An article I read on taming the inner critic suggested giving yourself a "woo-hoo" with every mistake. I've tried this, and it is more difficult to be hard on yourself after that. The true impact of celebration is learning, which also happens to be the true impact of failing.

To learn, we reflect on what we've done, what we've accomplished, how we got there, as well as what may have led to our mistakes, unfinished projects, and unmet goals. We can learn as much from our failures as our successes. To quote the movie "Chitty Chitty Bang Bang," "From the ashes of disaster, grow the roses of success." Isn't that something to celebrate?

What will you do to celebrate something big or small that you've accomplished?

Chapter Three

Never Finish Communicating

How We Let Others Treat Us

Just One Word

At the beginning of 2018, I tried a little something different for my New Year's resolution. I've set traditional resolutions in the past, but of course, they rarely stuck around past January. Then I tried setting goals for the year, but this practice wasn't the inspirational ritual I was looking for since I set goals regularly. So when I heard about a way to start the new year with beautiful simplicity, I had to try it.

Although the idea has been around for a while, it wasn't until the end of last year that I heard about one-word resolutions. The elegant minimalism of choosing one word to set as an intention for the year sums up who you want to be and how you want to live. This word directs your decisions, guides your goals, and streamlines all the jibber-jabber into a sticky, easy-to-remember focus of the year.

To get started, I thought a lot about which word to choose. I created lists of words that symbolized what I wanted to work on, what I wanted to accomplish, and mostly what I wanted to change to have a happier life. At the end of 2017 and the beginning of 2018, I was a ball of anxiety. I worried about everything. I constantly felt like the sky was falling; whether I was facing issues I could do anything to control or not. I was scared and super depressed. Not a place I wanted to be.

I shared my soul-crushing concerns at lunch with a dear friend and close adviser. As a visual example, I gripped the edge of the table with white knuckles and explained that was how I'd been feeling – like I was barely holding on. In a sweet, soft way, my friend laid the back of her hands on the table, cupped palms up, to help me understand that you can attract so much more in life from that position than in clutching for what is lacking.

We talked about letting go of what can't be controlled and trusting the Divine to provide solutions. From that conversation, I decided on "surrender" as my word for 2018.

The word "surrender" means a lot of things to me, but it certainly doesn't mean the same thing as "quit." I realized that the more I tried to force things to go the way I wanted, the worse my stress got, so I had to learn ways to stop worrying, focus on the things I could control, and trust everything would work out for the best. It wasn't easy.

I read a lot about letting go of worry and talked to many people about what they do to surrender stress. I worked with my therapist to change how my brain reacts to stressful situations and processes information with tools like EMDR, a treatment designed to help alleviate trauma. Meditation, visualization exercises, and a brainwave optimization app on my phone have also helped.

A turning point came when something happened that upset me quite a bit. Although the situation wasn't totally under my control, it happened because of a not so great choice I'd made. I got angry. I ranted. I cried. I wrung my hands. Then, I realized that at least I was clear about what was happening and could prepare to deal with the outcome.

I decided to "surrender" the situation and wait and see what happened. The minute I released my worry and anxiety, the perfect answer came to me in a flash, and I was able to act to avoid the situation completely. I could hear my inner wisdom by stilling the swirling mess of emotions and self-talk. It helped me understand what it felt like to let go of the stress. From that point forward, it's become much easier to stay calm and look for reasonable answers rather than catastrophizing and panicking.

Making "surrender" my year's focus helped in so many aspects of my life. In learning to let stuff go, I've gotten my spark back! Life is much happier, and all the things I was so worried about have worked out better than I expected. Framing "surrender" as a goal would have been tough, and I don't think I would have gotten as far working on this new skill. I know I still have a long way to go toward mastery, and there will be times when I have to remind myself to surrender, but the more I practice, the easier it gets.

Setting our resolution with one word

I'm totally sold on the one-word resolution. I encourage you to try this technique no matter which month you get started. It's not tough to do. Here are some tips.

Don't get in a hurry to pick your word.

You don't have to have your word by New Year's Day or even in January. Take a bit of time to do some soul searching to come up with the word that really means something to you.

Brainstorm a list.

There are many articles online to help you come up with your word, but to me, many of them overthink and overcomplicate it. So instead, think about what words have meaning for you to help you be the person you want to be to live your best life.

Narrow it down to one word.

There's a tendency to pick more than one word to fully explain what you mean, but don't do it. It splits the focus and makes it harder to make real progress. Instead, come up with a single word that best summarizes what you're thinking through the help of our friend, the thesaurus. Of course, you can make up your own mashup word if you can't find what you like.

The word's meaning can be complex and meaningful only to you.

The word I chose has several meanings for me that branch into more than one aspect of my life. To explain it to others at this point is complicated and probably only meaningful to me. I haven't distilled the concept down enough to explain it in a limited amount of words yet. That I fully understand my intention is what matters most.

This is all about you.

Don't pick a word about how you want others to act or how they treat you. If your concept relies on someone else's behavior or beliefs, it will not work. Basing our happiness on others' actions or how their beliefs align with ours is bound for failure since our behavior is the only thing we can even hope to control.

Keep your word in front of you.

Before I wrote this article, I checked in with the person who told me about this new way to make resolutions many months ago to find out she promptly forgot all about her focus after our conversation. After talking for a while, the word she chose came back to us. Although she didn't focus on it throughout the year, she has made good progress on her intention despite her forgetfulness. While the experiment may work by simply naming it, I believe that keeping the year's theme front and center in our lives will create more progress.

Be creative with it.

Remind yourself by creating a work of art around your word, designing a digital image, or simply writing your word down on an index card or sticky note. Put your visual reminder by your computer, car, mirror, journal, or other places you visit frequently.

Make it fun.

I read an article about a family who makes choosing their word a New Year's Eve tradition. They get together and create artwork around their word and share it with the rest of their family. The family members support each other throughout the year and help them make progress toward their focus. Whatever you can do to make it more fun for you – work it!

Just do it!

I hope you'll take the simple way to set your New Year's resolutions this year with one word. This technique works better for me than anything else I've tried, and it can work for you too. And – if you tell me your word, I'll tell you mine. Just email me at jill@finishingschoolformodernwomen. I'd love to hear from you.

What's your word?

What's on Your Front Burner?

"If your brain was a stove, what would be on your front burner?" While this is probably the worst pickup line I've ever heard, the woman's answer really floored me. She thought over the question for what seemed like an eternity as I held my breath to listen to her answer. When this young, conventional blonde beauty finally came up with a reply, it was, "I don't know...shopping?"

It's not that I never have "shopping" on my brain, but I wouldn't necessarily give it "front burner" status. Well, maybe occasionally. I'm not being judgy about anyone's priorities. I was just astounded at how long it took the woman to come up with that answer.

Yes, the question was weirdly worded, and we were in a bar, so it probably took a minute for her to translate it into, "What's topmost on your mind?" Perhaps she had her reasons for answering the question that way that had nothing to do with what was really on her mind, like dropping the hint that she's a material girl who craves alluring gifts.

Although this question seemed ridiculous to me at the time, it's interesting how often it still comes to mind. What indeed is on the front burner of my brain? I recently met with a brilliant woman who specializes in social media marketing. During the appointment, she mentioned that she's constantly reading articles and thinking about social media to stay updated with ever-changing technology trends. It made me think about what I'm spending my brainpower on.

So, I did a little audit and started paying attention to what I was paying attention to. It was enlightening. I found I spent way too much time reading the news and feeling anxious and overwhelmed about what was going on in the world. I've decided this isn't good for me because this nearly insatiable curiosity loop feeds anxiety. Just the thought of that makes my head hurt. Figuring that out has helped me decide which issues are most important to me and how I spend time.

I've always loved the Eleanor Roosevelt quote, "Great minds discuss ideas; average minds discuss events; small minds discuss people." It reminds me to be mindful of what I'm thinking about, listening to, and reading. Much like we are what we eat, we are also what we think. So here's what I'm going to spend more time thinking about.

I'm setting boundaries around what I'm mentally feeding myself.

The Finishing School has helped me realize that setting boundaries for myself is just as important as the boundaries I set for how I want to be treated by others. Rather than thinking of these boundaries as "rules," which don't get along well with my rebellious side, I'm thinking of them as self-care. I'm going to protect myself as much as I do everyone else I love.

For example, I'm limiting the amount of time I have to read news articles to 10 minutes at a time, rather than going from story to story for who knows how long. I'm also limiting the kind of information I'm paying attention to. For example, I won't watch programs or read books that are overwhelmingly, senselessly violent, or cruel. I already know that behavior is out there without putting those images in my brain.

I want to spend more time understanding others' realities.

We all live in our own reality bubble and see others through that lens. That's just how our brains work. If we let ourselves get too caught up in thinking that everyone's experiences and lives should live up to our own, it makes it hard to see anyone else's reality. Reading books like "The Color Purple" by Alice Walker and "The Good Earth" by Pearl Buck has helped me see life from other perspectives. Even better than reading is taking the risk to talk to actual people and engaging in uncensored discussions.

Recently I was asked to be on a panel for an International Women's Day/Race Relations event sponsored by Black Women Empowered. It was an enlightening experience. I was honored to have been a part of such an open, honest, and respectful discussion. There were about 50 engaged women and one man in the room, talking about racial divides and how we can come together to make all our lives better. Unfortunately, there are so many misunderstandings, myths, and lies we've all been told. We must listen to each other to move past this misinformation. We all left the event hungry for more dialogue.

Honored to be on a panel with these
powerful women

I want to be more intentional about where I put my focus.

When I was a kid, my cousins and I would randomly decide what to do when they came over. We'd make a list of the activities we wanted to play, then cut the list into strips and put them in the dryer. We'd tumble the options in the dryer like a giant bingo cage, and then someone would randomly draw a strip out of the dryer. We'd spend the next hour on that activity, picking a new idea when the time was up. It was a goofy, gameshow way to take turns, and it worked.

I'm going to try something similar now to be purposeful in where I put my focus. When an idea bubbles up that needs more attention, I'll write my thoughts on slips of paper and put them in a jar. Then, when I'm looking for something to do, I'll pull one of the ideas and go to work, just like having food ready to go when I'm hungry, rather than pulling into a fast-food drive-through. Instead of mindlessly binging on actions that don't take me closer to my goals, I'll have ideas ready to go.

I'm going to ask myself more questions.

I'm going to get more curious about what I don't understand and what makes me feel uncomfortable. So rather than setting issues aside, I can take time to think about what's happening and what it means to me. Writing down questions I'm pondering in a notebook and bullet-pointing answers is one of my favorite ways to think things through, plus I always feel better when I have a plan.

I think it's interesting that people get called out for "daydreaming." Some people believe that we're wasting time unless we're constantly in motion, working on something. But when we're in motion all the time, it's too easy to ignore the important stuff. Sometimes I feel guilty when I feel like I'm doing "nothing," but I remind myself that I am doing something. I'm thinking.

I'm going to pay more attention.

I'm going to ask others more questions too. I certainly don't have all the answers, but other people do. Who can help me better understand the questions I have? Who has expertise in what I want to learn? I've found that there's no faster way to get information than just talking to someone. These conversations often give me clarity or take an idea in a direction my brain would not have gone.

A big part of paying more attention is actively listening – to answers and opportunities. Intentionally listening to people shows them respect and helps them be more vulnerable to let you into their innermost thoughts. It also slows down the conversation to allow time to make meaningful connections and fully take in what the person said – not just what we want them to say.

Twenty percent of the energy we have available to use every day is taken up by the brain to keep our bodies running. As we learn new ways to think, the brain has to "work" to form new connections, using more precious energy. This brain drain is why learning can be exhausting. It's also why our brains try to "protect" us from change by ignoring what we don't want to hear and looking for information that reinforces the viewpoint we hold. By asking myself the question that seemed ludicrous when I heard it as a pickup line, I decide what information to put there and how to spend my brainpower.

What's on your front burner?

Speaking Our Voices

My favorite quote of all time is by historian Laurel Thatcher Ulrich from an obscure academic article she wrote in 1976.

"Well-behaved women seldom make history."

You may be able to tell I'm a bit of a rebel, so it's not too surprising that this quote is meaningful to me. But there's much more to it than that.

The biggest reason I love this quote is that it destroys the "good girl" myth. We're taught that "good" girls are passive, submissive, and compliant from the time we're children. We learn that our most important role is a "people pleaser" and that if we're good enough, we'll be rewarded. But, of course, this is absolute hogwash, especially from the people we expect to love us unconditionally.

We're told all kinds of things to beat down our initiative: "Don't draw attention to yourself." "Don't rock the boat." "Sit down and be quiet." "Get off your high horse." All these oppressive comments are meant to keep us silent and "in our place," to punish us for having the audacity to be visible. It is considered out of line to speak up for ourselves, and daring to be vocal gets labeled as being a "show-off," "nag," "hysterical," or worse.

It's no wonder we decide it isn't safe or worthwhile to speak our truth early in our lives.

These messages come from everywhere! They may have come from being scolded for speaking up when you were a kid or a boss or coworker who didn't appreciate your ideas. Unfortunately, these messages silence all of us. Can you pinpoint what situations convinced you to stop taking the risk?

Since I was a little girl, I've been accused of being sassy. But, of course, that didn't stop me. Now that I'm an adult, I'm sassy and proud of it! It all depends on the definition. To me, being sassy is about sharing an unpopular opinion, usually telling someone something they don't want to hear, which all circles back to breaking the "people pleaser" code.

These stifling experiences created the belief that speaking up would cause more pain. From this threat, we learned to withhold and question our voice throughout life. It's not that the people in these situations did this to hurt anyone. Often, they passed on what they'd been taught. Now the cycle repeats, passing along how we're expected to act and which parts of ourselves to keep invisible. We withdraw.

Withdrawing is how we protect ourselves from being hurt. We're safe as long as we play by the rules, don't ask too many questions, bring up too many hypotheticals, or give too many opinions. I see this every semester in the college class I teach. This belief makes it hard for most students to take risks to share what they're thinking. Especially when they see the class's response to the people who "over-share" (insert eye roll here) From a teaching standpoint, it's my mission to encourage the voices that are seldom heard.

What we learn in our early lives becomes engrained into our attitudes and beliefs as we grow. Even though it no longer serves us, we're convinced we need to protect ourselves as we did as children. We've learned to be afraid to speak our voice, so we don't get hurt.

However, in trying not to be hurt, we hurt ourselves by giving away our power and hiding our light.

What we all have to offer the world is so amazing, yet we doubt ourselves and let fear keep us from our purpose. I read an article several years ago about self-doubt and how selfish it is not to share our ideas. We think our opinions don't matter; our ideas are stupid. So we keep them to ourselves rather than sharing them with others. Maybe it's not always the next great breakthrough, but our ideas can reach beyond us to inspire others in ways we don't even realize. But not if we keep it to ourselves.

Understanding how we learned to avoid speaking our voice shines a light on where we are today. Looking at behaviors and attitudes that no longer serve us gives us the power to change them. For example, being reprimanded for acting "sassy" affected how I speak my voice. As a result, I had to redefine sassy into something positive – that I'm proud of today. I've learned how to express my voice positively from this knowledge, which helps me be heard rather than coming off as too salty.

The fear of being too confrontational is one of the biggest challenges in learning to speak our voice. To some people, "speaking our voice" means "telling it like it is" without considering the feelings of others by being hurtful or bullying. Most people don't want to live their lives communicating that way. So they don't say anything because they don't know how to have tough conversations constructively or are afraid of damaging relationships.

It takes practice.

Speaking our voice isn't something that comes naturally. Being a better communicator takes learning and practice. One of my favorite Finishing School classes is Tough Talks, where we talk about how to bring up uncomfortable topics and lose the fear of conflict to have productive confrontations. It's fun to watch people gain more confidence in learning to speak their voice respectfully.

It's all about boundaries.

We have a hard time giving ourselves permission to set limitations on how we want to be treated. The people pleaser in us doesn't want to disappoint others by saying "no." Unfortunately, there are people who know this and will take advantage of your good graces. Being "nice" and accommodating can cause us to accept things that don't deserve our tolerance.

Take a risk.

Silence and powerlessness go hand in hand. Telling our stories makes us human and shows the world through our eyes. When a person isn't affected by what's happening, it's human nature that they don't see or feel the impact until they're made aware. For change to happen, it takes people standing up and speaking the uncomfortable truths that no one wants to hear.

It is silence that has protected and emboldened predators, allowing many people to continue to be hurt over a long time. The history of silence is central to women's history, but we can't let oppression keep us quiet any longer.

Since words are often used to manipulate us, the more women challenge oppression, the harsher the criticism will become. It's not surprising that more laws are being passed to control women and that the strong women who speak up are getting condemned, harassed, and threatened. The Ulrich quote reminds me that making history is more important than "being nice" and how vitally important it is to speak our voices, be heard, and step into our power.

In what areas of your life can you speak your voice more powerfully?

Honor My Limitations

This week has been challenging. Not because anything bad happened, but because I've had to learn how to accept my limitations. And let me tell you, that does not come easy for me. I'd like to think I'm invincible and unstoppable and that I can power through anything by sheer will and determination.

Sure, I've had evidence this isn't true in the past. Like the time I came home from an Aveda sales conference, exhausted and scrambling to make up the lost time that happens after being out of town. During those years, in the pre-cell-phone era, I spent a lot of time pulling up to parking lot payphones. In a stressed-out stupor, I pulled up too close and at a weird angle to the phone on a pole.

When I went to drive away, I ended up wrapping my car around it instead. I still chuckle and roll my eyes, remembering getting out of the car, convinced I could push my nearly two-ton car sideways, away from the pole. I tried super hard to do it, too, until my muscles burned.

Thankfully a nice man watched me trying, and instead of laughing at me, he offered to help me navigate the car around the pole without doing too much more damage. I drove away red-faced, thinking, "Who do I think I am? Wonder Woman?"

It's not all bad, though. A lifetime of this kind of attitude has helped me achieve so much and be unafraid to take risks. In my consulting practice, this approach has also helped a lot of other people power through adversity and self-doubt to make their dreams a reality. However, this mindset has also cost me a lot physically, which I'm just starting to understand.

Years of life as a tough girl, shaking off injuries and walking off severe ankle sprains, have cost me a lot of cartilage, as it turns out. I've been rough with my body, ignoring pain and gritting my teeth to keep moving forward. The day of reckoning has arrived, and my body says, "¡No mas!"

To be fair to myself, I haven't totally ignored the pain. I've tried lots of things to help me limp through. I've been to an orthopedist and got anti-inflammatory medications and a Chinese medicine doctor for acupuncture and herbs. I've worn ugly orthopedic shoes and have had custom orthotics made to help position my foot to take advantage of the little cartilage remaining. I've iced it, worn an ankle brace, carried Biofreeze in my purse, and everything else I can do to keep walking. But I've noticed, especially in this cold weather, that what I've been doing isn't working as well. Something has changed.

So, I bucked up and went to my doctor to discuss what else we could do. We decided the next course of action is to see a podiatrist who specializes in ankles. As fate would have it, I helped a local podiatrist write a business plan and set up his private practice many years ago and was quite impressed with him. So we set up an appointment to see him right away.

What the doctor had to tell me was not good news. My ankle is "toast." He did an excellent job talking to me about my options. I'm not a candidate for stem cell injections that rebuild cartilage because I don't even have enough to build on anymore. The hard truth is that bone is rubbing against bone every time my ankle moves, causing a lot of inflammation and pain. Of course, losing weight could help.

There are cold laser therapy treatments to help reduce the inflammation that I may try first. Then there are ankle replacement surgeries, but they don't always help and wear out too fast.

I'm afraid my ballet days are over

The only long-term solution is holding the bone in place, either with a rigid brace or surgery, in other words, fusing the joint so my ankle won't move. I'm afraid this surgery will make it hard to walk without looking like a pirate with a peg leg. This does not please me.

I'm not telling you this story to get sympathy or an invitation to join my pity party. I'm writing this because I am really struggling with honoring my limitations, and I'm willing to bet I'm not the only one. Now that I'm taking a more head-on approach and talking to people about it, I'm processing what that means. Here's what I'm working on.

Swallow my pride.

When I went to Chicago for Christmas, I knew that walking around O'Hare Airport would hurt. Bad. When I flew home, my wise mother insisted I get assistance, which meant being pushed in a wheelchair to my gate. I was mortified, but I knew better than to ignore my mother, and besides, it hurt too bad to argue.

Talking to a friend when I got home, she told me she is the "Diva of the Airport" and is happily enthusiastic about being wheeled around, helping me realize it may not be too bad. I've got to say, getting through security was so much easier, and by the time I got to my gate, I wasn't completely exhausted. Still, when I got to Wichita, I ignored the person with the wheelchair waiting for me, too embarrassed that someone I knew might see me. I could barely walk by the time I finally made it to baggage claim.

Swallowing my pride to admit that I can't do everything is super hard for me. My parents tell me that when I was a toddler, and they asked if I needed help with something, I'd say, "No. I do it!" That stubbornness hasn't eased. Knowing how much it will hurt to do things and how difficult it will be to have a positive attitude once I get there keeps me away from events I would have energetically attended in the past. This isolation does not work with my social butterfly personality and leaves me feeling a bit more isolated than I'd like.

Ask for and accept help.

Not being completely self-reliant is also super hard for me. What has made it even harder to ask for help are the times people haven't lived up to what they told me they'd do. It disappoints me and affects how I feel about that person, especially if I've always come through for them. So, if I'm not afraid to take risks, isn't asking for help just another way of taking a risk?

Accepting help isn't just about the assistance I get from people. It's also about using tools to help me be in less pain. For example, after an excruciating week, I've been using a cane to help me get around. I'm getting a handicap placard for my car to park closer and not let it stop me from going where I want to go. Doing all this makes me feel incredibly vulnerable and old, but the alternative of being housebound stinks.

Take better care of myself.

Like most women, I've put other people before myself way too often. Weirdly, ignoring my injuries had a lot to do with not inconveniencing someone else. I'd like to think I'm getting better at learning to put myself first, but as I'm writing this, I realize that I still have so much to work on about saying "no."

The doldrums of winter are always challenging for me like they are for many other people I know – feeling overwhelmed and just raw. I need to remember to listen to my own advice when times get tough.

Accept it.

I've often said that it takes more strength to be "weak" than it does to be "strong." This saying is especially true in honoring our vulnerabilities. Because no matter how much I ignore or try to fight my limitations, the reality remains the same. My ankle is toast. Since I can't turn back time, I'm going to keep putting one foot in front of the other as long as I can, with all the help I can get, and love myself for persevering.

Rather than tough it out, how can you get help for what ails you?

Recovering

The struggle to make peace with my body and honor my limitations is real. I thought I'd made progress over the past year, but I realize now that although I thought I was taking better care of myself, it wasn't even close to enough. This year I've been forced to FACE my hurdles.

This isn't anything new. I've been hobbling around on a cartilage-free ankle for years. The choice of what to do about it came to an impasse this fall. Right before a big conference I co-chair, I amazingly broke my foot by merely walking over some soft ground.

Before I even went to the orthopedist to get my foot x-rayed, I knew the real issue was my ankle. The time had come when I had no choice but to fuse my ankle into one piece. Guess my ballet dancing days are over. I didn't want to do anything drastic because I thought it would limit my mobility. That excuse seems comical to me now that I realize how little mobility I had because of how painful it had become to walk.

A quick two weeks after I saw the orthopedist, I was scheduled for surgery. Getting ready to be off my feet for a couple of months without much time to prepare was challenging. Fortunately, the timing couldn't have been better since I was already stuck at home and working remotely because of the COVID shutdowns.

I had to figure out how to get around the house and take care of everything, including my beloved poodle. The littlest things we take for granted, like getting up my front steps or off the toilet without putting weight on one leg, became tremendous obstacles to overcome before surgery.

As if a broken foot wasn't enough, I came down with shingles right after the big, stress-filled conference! Thankfully, it was a mild case, but enough to know I'm getting the shots for shingles as soon as I'm fully recovered.

Thanks to family, friends, and my doctors, I got it all figured out in time. Friends loaned me medical equipment to make the little things more manageable. A friend organized a meal sign-up for me online, so people could schedule times to bring me food, pick up groceries, and do other errands. It was a godsend not to have to orchestrate all this myself.

Most beneficial, my mom came to town to be with me during surgery and stayed on for a few days after I got home to make sure I'd be alright on my own. She was a big help taking care of things around the house and teaching me how to get up from the floor when I fell off the knee-wheeler.

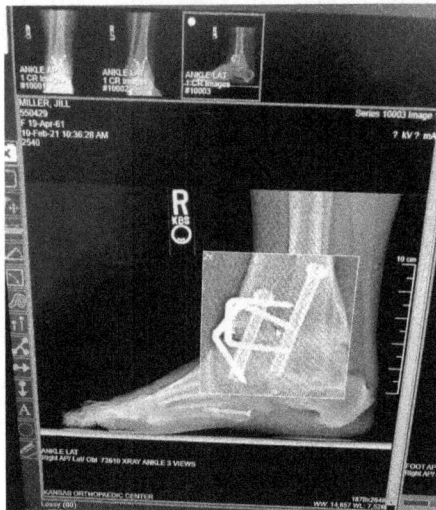

My new and improved ankle

The surgery went well, and I was making progress in my recovery, feeling stronger every day – when I had a significant setback. I was lying in bed, drinking hot tea and watching the British Baking Show, when I accidentally spilled boiling water down the outside of the same leg as my surgery. The pain from the surgery was nothing compared to the burn, which pain pills barely touched.

The boiling water was hot enough to cause second-and third-degree burns. This injury involved a visit to the burn unit and weekly follow-up appointments with a burn specialist to make sure I didn't need skin grafts! I felt like an idiot about injuring myself in such a stupid way; I only told a few people. I didn't mention it to my family until the burn doctor released me.

My leg healed, and it looks like there won't be any scarring. I know that all traces of the burn will disappear over time, but the pain and trauma of the experience are something I won't forget.

Since then, everything has been much better. I've recently graduated to a walking cast and can walk on two legs again. I'm immensely relieved and happy about that. It's hard to imagine how much we take for granted in living our everyday lives until something drastically changes. I have a new outlook on what it must be like to have limited mobility permanently.

What has surprised me the most about my healing adventure has been all the psychological stuff that comes with the physical. That has been the most challenging part of the experience for me. I thought I had a lot of these issues worked out! Maybe I've struggled with strong emotions because I've had a lot of quiet time by myself to think, or perhaps it's just part of the healing process.

I've learned to make peace with asking for and accepting help. I'm so used to being the caregiver; it doesn't feel right to be the one that needs care. I've been forced to face the reality of living by myself as I age and what that means for the future.

I also had to learn to let go of some of the workloads I put on myself to focus on healing. It took unimaginable amounts of energy to get around to do even the simplest tasks, never mind the energy the body needed to heal.

Every time I tried to write, I couldn't make myself do it. I had some great classes lined up that I didn't have the energy to market or teach, so I quietly canceled them. It hasn't been easy, but now that I've dug deeper into these issues, I'm grateful to have a better understanding of myself and the growth that's come with it.

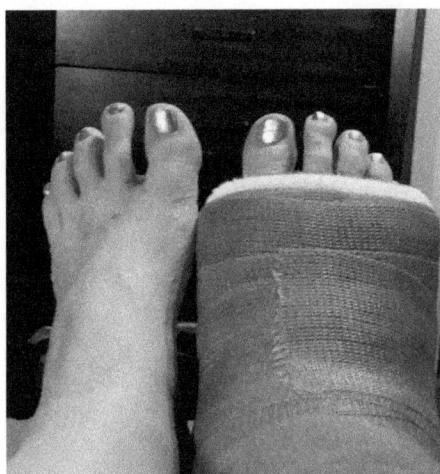

Not my idea of stylist footwear

Next week I go to the orthopedist to get my cast off. I'll be wearing a boot for I don't know how long, but this is an exciting step toward recovery. I'm hoping it won't be long before I can drive a car again. Even though I've had a ton of help from my friends, I miss the independence of going where I want by myself.

Now that I'm feeling more myself, I'm ready to move out of survival mode and decide what's next. Thankfully, my business consulting practice has been so busy during the recovery that I haven't had much get-up-and-go for anything else.

It takes a lot out of a person to be in pain all the time. I am super excited for what life will be like to walk now that every step won't hurt so much. Now that I have more energy, I want to be more thoughtful about using this precious resource in the future.

I'm not sure what the future will hold. I'm going to take some time to decide. But, it seems like the right timing to hit the reset button and do some more reinvention.

What pains are your procrastinating?

Boundaries Are Love

I went to an Alternative and Holistic fair because I wanted to talk to an intuitive medium who had read my cards when I was in my 30s. I saw she would be there, so I had to go. She told me something a long time ago that had stuck with me, and I wanted to see what she had to say this time.

I didn't tell her anything, but she was amazingly spot-on about what was going on in my life now, with no big surprises. When she asked me if I had any questions, I went for the trite one I bet she gets all the time, "Do you see any romance in my life?"

She laughed and looked me in the eye with an expression of disbelief and said, "You're not even trying!" I admitted she was right. She went on to tell me, "Why fix what's not broken? You are the most content and happy that you've ever been in your life. Why do you want to mess that up?" I still laugh when I think about how incredibly right she was.

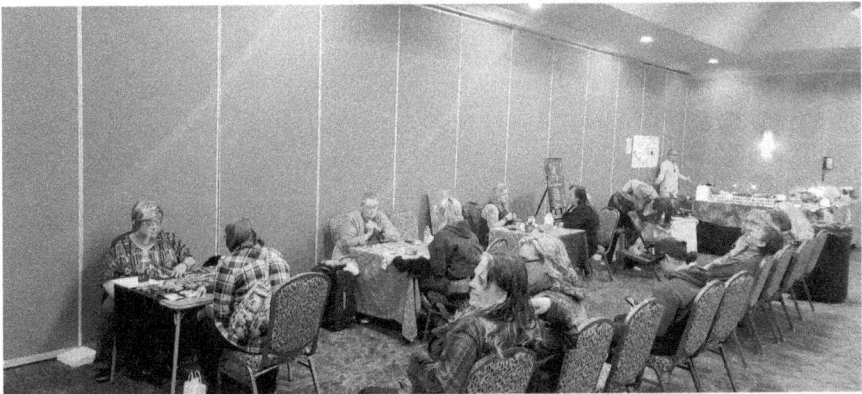

Waiting for my appointment

February always makes me think about the lack of a romantic relationship in my life. Not only is Valentine's Day ever-present, but it's also the anniversary of the momentous occasion when I freed myself from the bonds of unholy matrimony and a very toxic relationship. These arbitrary dates in our lives remind us that it's time to reflect on our annual progress. It's tiresome – and healing.

When these anniversaries come up, it can feel like we're revisiting the same old crapola. But I've learned to think about this differently. It's not going back; it's about spiraling inward to dig deeper. My friend Janet calls it the Slinky Effect. Each time we revisit past trauma, we uncover more. We peel back another layer of our soul armor like an onion to find the treasures inside.

Several years ago, I decided that rather than ruminate over lost love, I'd spend the energy devoting the month of February to celebrate a different kind of love. As a survivor of trauma, I've spent the past seven years working on healing and learning to love myself. Now I feel the love – and that's something to celebrate!

I know this sounds weird, but I am happily in a committed relationship with myself. Huzzah! And yeah, I don't want to mess that up by leaving myself for someone else.

As I've pondered self-love lately, questions have popped up. Do survivors of trauma have a more challenging time learning to love themselves than people without PTSD? Are there any unicorns out there that haven't experienced trauma? It probably doesn't matter how hard it is. There's no getting around the truth that learning to love yourself is a big part of healing.

Still, sometimes I wonder if what I'm really doing is trying to protect myself. By not taking any risks in romantic relationships, I can guarantee I won't get hurt – or worse than that, put myself back into a toxic relationship with someone else.

Honestly, this scares the daylights out of me. I question if I can trust myself to see the pink and red flags that warn me I'm being ripened for picking by an abusive personality. Narcissists love me, so this isn't an unreasonable fear. I've been fooled before.

At the "Love Yo Self" Finishing School
Workshop

So what can we do to get started on this quest for self-love? So much of the advice on how to maneuver this journey feels out of touch and uninspiring. For example, gratitude journals and telling yourself "I love you" are helpful, but they aren't enough. As I considered how to protect myself without hiding from the world, I had a stunning realization.

The biggest act of self-love is setting boundaries.

Because to be successful in setting boundaries, we must know and ask for what we want. When we've been taught to believe we're not worthy of having a voice, through abuse or general repression, even knowing what we want becomes a struggle.

I started the Finishing School for Modern Women because I know how hard it is to stand up for ourselves. So I've made it my mission to help women "own their power," and I reinforce this concept in every class I teach. Now I realize that what I've been calling "owning your power" is actually self-love.

Setting restrictions around how I want to be treated and learning to communicate these borderlines is not easy. For example, I've decided my friendships need to be equal in how much I give and take in a relationship. It isn't easy to let someone you love know that you need more from them and stop coming to their rescue the minute they cry for help. It has taken me years of deliberate work, and I'm far from mastering this art. Nevertheless, here's what I'm learning.

Boundaries are your personal policy about what is acceptable.

Remember that boundaries are set to control our own behavior, not someone else. It's not something we do "to" people. Also, our policies will vary depending on whom we're interacting with.

Spend some time in self-reflection.

To successfully introduce and set boundaries, it's key to understand why these behaviors are essential to you and how they'll benefit your emotional well-being.

Start simply.

When you don't have many boundaries in place, the thought of adding them may seem overwhelming. Build up slowly and take some time to reflect on how each boundary is working.

Be gentle at first.

People who don't set boundaries don't like it when you set them for yourself. It may take easing them into this new reality and for you to get used to communicating what you want. Keep calmly practicing, and it will get better.

Create boundaries for yourself.

What will you put into place for your own behavior? For example, you can set definite work hours, especially if you work from home or are a workaholic like me. The more you set and uphold the boundaries you put in place with yourself, the easier it is to do with others.

Keep them simple.

Keep boundaries simple and clearly define what acceptable and unacceptable behavior you expect from yourself and others. Remember, you don't have to explain or justify your decisions.

Set them right away.

Learning to set boundaries gets more complicated in pre-existing relationships, so communicate them in new relationships straight away. By setting boundaries and expectations from the beginning, everyone knows where they stand, which can cut back on feelings of hurt and confusion.

Talk about it.

Communication is vital in the world of boundaries, especially if someone consistently oversteps yours. Even though you might need to raise your concerns, these discussions don't need to be confrontational. Instead, let people know how they can work within your boundaries. For example, the hours you *are* available for appointments.

Be consistent.

Standing by your boundaries sometimes and letting them slip other times sends mixed messages and are confusing.

Instead, speak up each time someone pushes your limits and remind them of your requests.

Take it slow.

If you need to compromise, be flexible and take it slowly. It isn't unreasonable to negotiate boundaries and might be a clue that your boundaries are too rigid. But, never agree to anything that doesn't feel right, or you don't intend to live by.

Be your biggest advocate.

For boundaries to have a strong foundation, you're got to show yourself some love. To put limitations in place that protect you, you must believe that you deserve the respect you're asking for. You must be as protective as a Mama Grizzly Bear for yourself as much, if not more than you are for others you love.

You are worthy of adoration. Love yourself and let others know how they can show you love too.

What boundary can you set for yourself or others that will bring you more peace and happiness right away?

Chapter Four

Never Finish Adapting

How We Are When Times Are Hard

1. Come in Off the Ledge

2. The Struggle Is Real

3. Life or Death

4. Holiday Blues Survival

5. Pity Party

6. Kick-Ass

7. Thriving Through Chaos

Come in Off the Ledge

Masking up

Maybe you've noticed. There's a lot of craziness going on out there. The spread of COVID that started in March 2020 has us all upset and confused about what to do. Everything feels eerily surreal since we've been sequestered in our homes for the past two months.

With hospital ICUs already at capacity and shortages of medical supplies and equipment, communities around the globe are shutting down and people are staying home. Here at home, our governor announced that school would be closed starting May 17 and not to come back after spring break.

On March 30, a state-wide stay-at-home order directed everyone to only go out for "essential activities," like getting food or medical help. Except for these "essential businesses," everything is shut down. Meetings must be held outside, "provided individuals maintain a distance of six feet from one another and abide by the 10-person limitation on gathering size."

People are scared and angry. Armed to the teeth, protesters are storming government buildings to fight the mask mandates and other safety precautions the public health authorities are pleading with the legislators to enact. Crazy conspiracy theories about where the disease came from and how to stay safe are swirling around. And on top of all this, general overall feelings of anxiety are hanging in the air. It feels like we're going off the deep end. It's nuts and all too much.

So, rather than getting caught up in these drama cyclones, I invite you to come in off the ledge with me. Take some deep breaths and check out these tips.

Try not to obsess about the news.

When I start my morning by reading the news and checking social media, it wrecks my mood for the whole day. It stresses me out to read about the crazy, self-obsessed things people are doing, and that's frustrating and exhausting. Doom scrolling is addictive, so rather than spending free time on the news, try to focus on living your life and what is within your control. Most importantly – don't read the comments on social media posts. (I need to listen to my advice on this one!)

Don't believe the hype.

Some factions purposely share misinformation to keep us confused, divided, and fighting. They're posting at record levels. A recent Pew Research Center study showed nearly two-thirds of Americans say they've seen news and information about COVID that seemed completely made up.

The horrible thing about the floods of troll-farm manipulation is that when people share these conspiracies, the messages gain traction and become louder and louder – so much so that it drowns out the truth. So it's our job to protect the health of our community by making sure the news sources are credible before passing them on, even when they agree with your worldview.

Look for the good.

Even though you can't tell it from reading the news, there is more "good" than "bad" out there. Most of us agree on more things than we disagree on when we come together and talk. It's easy to let the negativity suck up all your attention and emotional bandwidth, so try focusing on the positive things - outside and inside your life. The list of all the things I'm grateful for during this pandemic is vast. That you're reading this article is big on my gratitude list.

This is not the "new normal."

It's going to be a while before we can go to what we were doing before the pandemic, but eventually, we will be able to hug again, go to concerts, meet friends for day drinking in real life, and all the other things we're missing.

To call this isolation the "new normal" feels like settling for something that isn't even close to good enough. Until we can learn more about COVID and understand how to treat it, we're in an adapting phase. This ever-changing understanding is why things are changing so fast. Having to pivot so often is exhausting and takes a lot of brain cells to make happen. It's time to put on our thinking caps and rev up our creative problem-solving engines to keep moving forward. Here's hoping vaccinations can take us closer to some stability.

Feel all the feels.

In case you didn't notice, people have been more emotional than usual as the pandemic continues. I know I am. I can barely watch a toilet paper commercial without crying. Vacillating between anger, sorrow, happiness, and frustration is expected. Whether we want to admit it to ourselves or not, we are in the middle of a public health crisis.

People who have never been depressed are depressed now. And for a good reason. There will be good days, bad days, and everything in between. So be gentle with yourself and give yourself some time and space to experience *all* your emotions.

Kindness goes a long way.

There's nothing like little acts of kindness to make a day, yours or someone else's. Empathy is especially important now. I love the stories about the Kansas farmer who sent his spare N95 mask to New York City first responders and the 11- year-old girl who wrote a thank you letter to her mail carrier. These feel-good stories keep us all going. Even something as small as calling someone to check in on them and let them know someone is thinking about them helps. The best reason for doing something kind for someone else is how incredible it makes you feel too.

Reach out for help if you need it.

Sometimes reaching out for help from a friend or family member is all you need. When I start to feel lonely, I give someone a call. But other times, you need more help than they can provide. Here are some resources with thoughtful people waiting to help you:

National Domestic Violence Hotline, (800) 799–7233
National Suicide Prevention Lifeline, (800) 273-8255
Suicide and Crisis Lifeline, call or text, 988
Crisis Text Line, 741741

Give yourself a hug.

While sequestered, we're missing human connections outside our homes. Try giving yourself a hug. Put your arms around yourself, give a little squeeze, and send yourself some love. It may sound cuckoo, but studies show hugs are universally comforting and are essential to our overall health. Besides, it feels good!

What adaptations did you make during the pandemic that you've incorporated into your life since?

The Struggle Is Real

I always know the end of summer is coming when I hear the cicadas' song. This insect always has both terrified and fascinated me. They look primeval, and their significant size and the loud, crazy sound they make are intimidating. They must be more bark than bite because I've never heard of anyone being hurt by this big bug. My brave protector, Jack Poodle, will snatch them out of the air and make a snack of them so I know they aren't toxic.

Starting a new life, this time with wings

I can imagine how the cicadas must feel before they shed their shell. We're nearly six months into the pandemic, and while some restrictions are slowly starting to lift, I'm starting to feel a cooped-up itchiness in my spirit. I've got to be honest with you – I'm struggling. I'm ready to burst out of my shell. I've missed my people, going out together, celebrating, physical touch, travel, and life.

I think we're all struggling right now, which may be why society feels like it's about ready to detonate. We're all operating in a state of chronic stress. No matter how hard we try to adapt and keep a positive outlook, the underlying tension is simply too much.

We're mourning the events we traditionally made part of our yearly routine, like graduations, family reunions, and birthday celebrations. While it's painful to think about what we're missing, acknowledging and mourning these lost rites of passage can be therapeutic.

The anxiety I'm feeling from all the anger and unrest is getting to me too. Watching the unnecessary violent clashes between peaceful protesters and government militia hurts my stomach. The rage and misinformation around the Coronavirus and the wearing of masks are disheartening. When we should all be coming together to slow the spread of the illness and get through this crisis, we're moving further apart.

We need more loving-kindness in the world. But unfortunately, the nasty ways we react to stress are human nature. When people are stressed, they tend to lash out, showing the ugliest part of their personalities. I'm having a hard time not judging people for the arrogant ignorance and disregard some are showing for our fellow humans.

I read something recently that helped me. One of my favorite business authors, Mark W. Schafer, says, "Just care for people. Love people. Stop judging others. When you judge people, you don't have time to love them."

Having to learn new ways of doing what we used to take for granted is taxing too. School is getting ready to start, stirring up even more controversy about how to keep students and teachers safe. When the world erupts into chaos, it's not realistic to think we can achieve all the activities at the same levels as before. Students weren't meant to be cooped up in front of a screen all day, and we can't expect them to retain all the information they could in a classroom.

The exhaustion from all the tragedy and loss is mounting up too. I heard the term "Pandemic Burnout" recently, and while I didn't know it was a thing, I know how it feels all too well. Over the past few months, I feel like my life has been busier and more stressful than usual. Something has got to give. Now that I know burnout is to blame for feeling drained, it is time to acknowledge this condition and act on it.

I'll be heading back to school soon myself. I teach Entrepreneurship in the Arts at Wichita State University in the fall and have 22 students enrolled to take it already. So before class starts, I have to decide how to make this class meaningful for my students. Fortunately, classes online through the Finishing School for Modern Women have helped me prepare and learn what I'll need to make hybrid classes work.

As if all the extra stress going on in the world right now isn't enough, life continues to happen. In April, I found out that my baby brother, Michael, was diagnosed with advanced-stage metastatic cancer. He began chemotherapy but reacted to the medication, and they're trying to figure out what to do next. So how do I process that amid everything else?

What happens for me is that it gets pushed down, its heaviness always under the surface. I've practiced the art of denial for so many years, and I'm pretty good at it. Worrying about things I can't control is a distraction, so I try not to let my mind go there. I also know from practice that denial causes depression, and I'm teetering right on the edge. Surrendering these feelings isn't easy, and I'm trying.

My family is close, and we all want to come together when something happens. Unfortunately, we can't do that right now. I had to threaten my Mom to keep her from making a nearly 1,000-mile road trip to her son during a pandemic. I worry the most about my parents and how they're coping. I'll take all the love and prayers you can send our way.

In the meantime, I'll be listening to the cicadas. Except for this year, I'm rethinking what this bellowing bugs' song symbolizes to me. I've realized the story of cicadas is one of rebirth. These nymphs spend most of their lives underground, lying dormant until it's time to make an appearance. Then, they crawl up from the earth to find somewhere safe to attach themselves to shed the shell of their past – and fly into the future. Their emergence brings me hope that we'll do the same thing ourselves soon when we crawl out from this pandemic.

What brings you hope?

Life or Death

Sometimes things change at lightning speed, especially when it comes to life and death.

The Thursday evening in late July was beautiful. Storms across the state had cooled the temperature down, and a lovely, gentle breeze made it feel even better. Just the kind of evening my miniature rescue poodle, Jack, and I like to hang out at the dog park. It's stress-reducing for me to go to the park, laugh at the goofy dogs, and talk to the other weird dog people while getting some fresh air. Jack loves getting out of the house to see his doggie friends.

That evening quite a few dogs were running around and having fun. It seemed like a pretty mellow evening. Dogs were coming over to Jack, introducing themselves in the usual sniffing each other kind of way. We hadn't been there 5 minutes when one of the get-to-know-you-dosey-dos turned ugly.

Things can go from hunky-dory to death in a heartbeat.

One minute we were having fun; the next minute, one of the bigger, mixed-breed dogs attacked Jack. Viciously. And would not back down. Dogs are such pack animals that others joined in as soon as one dog started attacking Jack. People came running to get their dogs, but it's not easy with a frenzy like that going on, and dogs won't listen to their owner's commands.

I tried to grab Jack but couldn't reach him. I recognized Jack's cries rising out of the tussle as he was hurt. I didn't know what to do: how close to get into the middle of the fray. I kept thinking they'd break apart, the way it usually happens when dogs get into fights at the park. But, the attacking dog wouldn't stop going after my baby.

Sometimes putting yourself in harm's way is the only way to get things done.

When I heard a woman scream in a nearly hysterical voice, "He won't let go." I knew I had to act immediately. People were trying to pull the dogs apart, which I knew would cause more injury.

I threw myself to the ground, forced the dog's teeth apart, and pried his jaws off my little man. It must have taken a lot of strength because my shoulders and upper arms burned for days. I found bruises on my hands and scratches on my arms and feet that I didn't even feel while I was in shock.

I was lucky. I could have gotten bitten. Bad.

Recovering

Just because you act like a badass doesn't mean you are one.

Jack wasn't completely innocent in this incident. He wants to be the alpha and growls at dogs that he doesn't want to sniff him. The bigger dogs usually look at him like he's crazy and leave him alone. But, unfortunately, the one on Thursday night didn't back down.

After we got the dogs apart, people started yelling at the attacking dog's owner, telling him his dog had been aggressive since they got there and needed to leave the park immediately. The owner asked for my phone number and promised to call me, but he never did. I don't expect he will. I just hope he stays away from the park and thinks twice about letting his dog around others.

Emergency rooms are the same, whether they're for dogs or people.

Many people at the dog park advised me to go straight to the vet multiple times. Duh! Looking Jack over when I got to my car, it miraculously appeared that he wasn't seriously injured. His skin was ripped apart in about a three-inch gash in his right armpit, but there didn't seem to be any other damage, and there wasn't much bleeding. He was definitely in shock, we both were, but he was quiet and calm. It took me a few minutes to calm down enough to remember where the emergency vet clinic was and how to get there. It seemed like we were driving through molasses, taking way too long to get there.

Emergency rooms take a lot of patience, and a clinic for animals is no exception, especially since we only have one in town. Waiting is tough, and since Jack's injury wasn't life-threatening, I knew it would be a while before he could see a doctor.

We were put in an exam room right away, and a quick preliminary exam assured me it was only a flesh wound. We were in that cold, white, quiet room for a long time, feeling the pain from our boo-boos more and more as the shock wore off. Eventually, they took Jack to stitch him up and sent me home to wait. It was 1 AM when I finally carried my zonked-out poodle in our front door.

Advocate for those who can't and don't take "no" for an answer.

Even with the pain meds, Jack let me know he was still in pain and whined and cried as the sedative wore off. It broke my heart. After a night of crying, a friend encouraged me to call the vet to increase his medication the following day.

It took a surprising amount of persistence to get this done. Following up with Jack's usual vet would involve an office visit, which couldn't happen until Monday. Rather than giving up on getting Jack relief over the weekend, I called the emergency clinic and explained the situation. Thankfully they conceded to give us a prescription. The Poodle rested much more comfortably, and I was even able to get some sleep.

There are good people in the world.

I was deeply touched by the response Jack and I got on Facebook. In less than 24 hours, 205 people reacted, and 103 commented on the post I put up while we were waiting at the clinic. That doesn't count the numerous phone calls, texts, and Facebook messages offering to come and sit with me, checking to see if I needed anything.

I cried like a baby when I got the message from a friend that she had gone to the clinic and paid half the bill. She told me that I do so much to help other people and that it was my turn. I still tear up about it every time I think about it. It's all overwhelmingly touching.

Our furry friends are so much more than a pet.

The relationship we have with our four-legged friends is profound. They're more than a friend, more than a family member – we are connected at the soul. The unconditional love they show us is something we can't begin to understand or imitate. They learn everything about us, understand us, and love us anyway.

I rescued Jack four years ago when he was abandoned as a puppy by his owner. But he really rescued me. He came into my life when I was newly single and rebuilding who I was after decades of being in a bad marriage. He is my confidante, constant companion, cheerleader, true love, and my rock. So when I realized he might die, I didn't think twice about prying him out of the jaws of death. I am so grateful that we both made it through that terrifying experience without more severe injuries. I don't even want to think about how it could have turned out.

We took the weekend to chill together. Jack requested extra TLC and cuddles, and I think he knows I saved his life. Considering what he has done for my life, I'm happy to oblige.

Give your furry friends extra love.

What can you do right now to show the ones you love how much they mean to you?

Holiday Blues Survival Guide

We've always been led to believe that the holidays are a joyous, magical time of year. A time when families come together, and everyone is happy, happy, happy, and – if you're good – miracles happen. Wouldn't it be wonderful if that's the way it is for everyone? But, unfortunately, it isn't. I don't mean to be a buzz-kill here, but it's true. Life is not a Hallmark movie, and for many people, this can be a sad, lonely, upsetting time of year – for lots of reasons.

I imagine that all of us, over the lingering course of our lives, have had stellar and not-so-stellar holidays. Sometimes the memories and disappointments can be so painful or off-putting that they overshadow the spirit of the season. So instead of all the Christmas hype making us feel excited about what's to come, it puts us in a not so festive funk.

To make it worse, markers in time, like holidays and the beginning of a new year, cause us to reflect on what has happened in our lives since last year. While I think it's important to celebrate where we've been and think about where we're going, it is not helpful to compare ourselves to others or even to other times in our life.

Situations change. There will always be highs and lows, and no promises things will be better in the new year. But these hills and valleys are what it takes to learn, keep growing, and ask ourselves the hard questions.

I still believe in Santa and the magic of
Christmas

I'm one of those weird people who likes Christmas. I've even been known to listen to Christmas music at other times of the year. That weird. I have many good memories from my childhood that still seem magical when I think of them, like the aroma of making peanut brittle in Grandma's kitchen.

Still, some years I'm just more into the festivities than others. Life doesn't just stop because it's the holidays. It just means there's more to try to jam into every day. I must admit, I've been ignoring it this year, only doing the bare minimum of my traditions that I feel like doing.

I've learned that the fastest way for me to resent the festivities is to do things just because I think I should, rather than because I want to. I'm looking at the holidays as a chance to relax and take a little break, so the easier I can make things for myself, the better. That includes decorating and making peanut brittle.

The holidays can be tricky, and it doesn't help that it's getting dark too early. The gloomy days stir up the winter blues for those afflicted. Whether your Christmas is white or blue, here are some suggestions to help you.

Take care of yourself.

Being busy to the point of feeling overwhelmed usually means we're taking care of everything but ourselves – even the super basic stuff, like postponing potty breaks for no good reason. While it seems like no big deal, ignoring this body function causes urinary tract infections, kidney stones, incontinence, and more! I'm guilty of it myself.

I'm also bad about going all day on no fuel, not eating a decent meal, and wondering why I feel so wrung out at the end of the day. When I'm feeling stressed, I ask myself a question I learned from Sarah Ellen, one of our co-teachers at the Finishing School for Modern Women, "What do I need right now?" Do I need to eat? Walk around the block? Take a nap? Don't ignore the signals our bodies send us, and take care of your needs. We make our own magic.

Revisit what makes you happy.

Hopefully, you have some magical Christmas moments from childhood that you can revisit. What seemed magical to you? For me, memories of making peanut brittle with my grandma was something I revisited last year. She cranked out so much every year it felt like she was supplying Santa! The smells, tastes, and even the sugar burns take me back to being in the kitchen with Grandma, creating that magic all over again.

Let someone else do the work.

I love Christmas lights but don't have the time, energy, and gumption to put on a big light show. However, I love that other people do, so a fun part of Christmas for me is driving around and looking at the lights. I'm also lucky to have overachiever neighbors who stretch their display onto my house. They've made a 5-foot wooden cut-out of the Grinch that stands on my roof, pulling the lights off their house. I couldn't love it more.

Remember, you're in charge.

There isn't anything you absolutely HAVE to do, especially when it comes to Christmas. Don't feel like dragging out all the decorations and setting everything up, only to take it down a few weeks later? Don't. Since I decided I don't need to do this every year, my life has gotten much more relaxed during the holidays. Depending on what I have going on, I can choose how spartan or Liberace I want to go. So pick your favorites and forget the rest.

Practice your boundaries.

You're in charge of what you will and won't be part of. Setting boundaries and communicating them to others about how you'll participate and expect to be treated is the secret to happiness and self-esteem. You don't have to go to three or four gatherings in a day unless you want to. You can opt-out of anything and everything you want.

By the way, visiting people, even family, who are toxic is not required of you. Just because it's Christmas doesn't mean they'll be any nicer or easier to deal with. You have my permission. Just don't.

Celebrate the ones you miss.

One of the things that makes it sadder this time of year is thinking of the loved ones that won't be with us. Their absence can make it feel like celebrating is not appropriate or worthwhile.

I know I will miss my friends Myrna, Rose, and Sharon at the Heifer Christmas Party this year. I already am. So, I've decided not to ignore how I'm feeling and honor and celebrate the losses to the herd of this women's group I love being part of.

I plan to recognize these women in a way that honors their unique contributions to the world and our club. I'll break into spontaneous singing for Myrna, and I'll make funny, snarky comments for Rose. Sharon made us all mix CDs of her favorite songs every year for Christmas. To celebrate and honor her, I plan to listen to last year's gift and reminisce about the trouble we stirred up together. While I'll still miss my spirited friends, celebrating them makes me feel like they're still within me.

You're not in it alone.

Last year, I over-extended myself in too many ways, throwing me into a dark place and stealing my sparkle for months. I'm not doing that again. This year, I plan to thrive rather than survive the holiday blues by acknowledging and working on what I'm feeling. Thriving will require setting boundaries for me – balancing my workaholic tendencies with my social butterfly necessities and downtime at home to recharge my batteries and love on the poodle. It also means not trying to do this alone, knowing that people who love me want to help and support me.

What can you do this year to make your holiday brighter?

Pity Party

I do love a party

Alright, Modern Women. I have a confession to make. I've been depressed. Some days it's all I can do to not act like a toddler throwing themselves on the ground, kicking and screaming in a full-blown fit.

This funky feeling hits me every February like clockwork. Welcome seasonal depression, otherwise known as Seasonal Affective Disorder (SAD), if you're fancy. Yes, this bonafide mood disorder affects over 10 million Americans and is four times more common in women than men. Go figure.

I'm not getting enough exercise, eating a lot of comfort food, working way too much – and generally not taking good care of myself. Since I'm a natural extrovert, one of the worst ways the Winter Blues hits me is isolation, or "avoidance of social situations." I want to stay home and wallow in my pity party, and I can come up with plenty of justifications to do just that.

I know I'm not the only one. I have lots of friends that suffer, and I do mean suffer, with this affliction too. I know that I probably won't see much of these people until spring, and that's okay. We still keep in touch and occasionally check in with each other, knowing that it won't be long before the sun comes back again. We don't take it personally. If you're one of the millions affected by this, you know what I mean.

While SAD isn't much different than your garden variety depression, it is thought to be related to the amount of melatonin in the body, a hormone that regulates sleep. As the winter days get shorter, we go into hibernation mode and merely want to hide out in our caves. There is a theory that people sensitive to SAD may produce less Vitamin D, which is believed to produce serotonin, a major neurotransmitter involved in mood swings.

Since I'm not planning to move somewhere sunnier anytime soon, I've got to own this and take some steps to cope with it. Wallowing in depression doesn't help; in fact, it makes things worse. Feeling hopeless makes us feel powerless.

Pity Parties are okay for a little while, but the longer I'm stuck there, the harder it is to get out. So I purposely work on actions to help myself through the season.

Here are some things I'm working on to help me feel better.

Admit it.

One of the first things I have to do when I'm depressed is to admit it to myself. I don't want to look at it, just like a dog that won't look at you when they've done something they know is bad. But, I've learned that the sooner I can acknowledge my emotions, the better I feel. One of my biggest aha's from the past year is that emotions aren't "good" or "bad." They're just emotions that need to be examined rather than ignored. These feelings won't consistently ease up until we take a closer look.

Clean house.

It's incredible how much better I feel when my house is clean. It doesn't have to be the entire house. Just the room I'm wallowing in helps change my mood. It seems more like self-care to me than a chore. Sometimes, mindless, mundane tasks feel good and work off some nervous energy.

Reach out.

I don't have to actually "go" anywhere to be less isolated. Calling a friend on the phone, or even exchanging text messages, is a way to have some human connection. I'm lucky to have friends who will let me vent when I need to and don't expect me to be "positive" all the time. Of course, I reciprocate when they need it too.

Make a play date.

Intentionally make an appointment with a friend to get out of the house and do something fun. It can be as low-key as meeting at the dog park or a museum. It seems that food or drinks are the go-to for get-togethers, but I need something a little more active right now.

Move around.

The endorphins from exercise significantly lighten moods. When it's freezing, I have a hard time getting motivated to go to the gym, especially since water exercise is my jam. One of my favorite ways to get moving in the winter is to play Dance Party! I play my favorite, uplifting music and dance like no one's watching – except the Poodle.

Go to a movie.

Movies are low-key, and I can go by myself if I don't feel like coordinating with a friend. It gets me out of the house, and I can escape into another world for a couple of hours. I intentionally seek out happy or exciting movies, not tear-jerkers!

Get extra pet lovies.

Jack Poodle may have seasonal depression too. Maybe he's

just sensitive to how I feel, or he's feeling cooped up too, but he gets extra clingy. I make sure to give him some devoted cuddle time several times a day. It makes us both feel better.

Get help.

One of the things I'm working on this year is learning to ask for and accept help. I'm involved in many things, maybe too many things, and it becomes super overwhelming since I stink at asking for help. I think this contributes to being depressed. Keeping all the plates spinning all the time isn't humanly possible, even though I expect that of myself.

In the throes of depression, sometimes it seems like it would be a relief to give up and let all the plates crash to the ground. But, realistically speaking, that's not an option. Figuring out where I need help and how to get it takes energy, time, and insight. I called a meeting of my closest advisers, my Worthy Women Club, to help me figure out how to get the help I needed.

Don't be afraid to talk about It.

In talking to my friends, I find that I'm not the only one feeling like this. A bunch of us have had our own private Pity Party. Maybe we should get together for a big, pajama dance party blowout. We realize we're not the only ones when we talk about it together, which helps a little. My friends don't expect me to be my usual perky self all the time and are understanding when I'm down.

Also, depression is a liar. Sometimes it's hard to tell what's real and what isn't. Talking to someone about what's eating you will give clarity and hope. Speaking to the people I'm close to has been my safety net. A good therapist is a wonderful thing too, and I'm lucky to have an incredible one.

Take advantage of sunny days.

When it is a sunny day, like today, get outside! Absorbing the Vitamin D from the sun helps, even if it's still chilly out.

The Poodle and I are headed outside. We both need it!

What do you do to get through the winter blues?

Kick Ass

I wish I had met Cindy Cushing Coughenour, the founder of Fearless and Female when I was much younger. The first time I saw her in action was at the Peace, Love, Safety event in 2016, an evening of self-defense, food, fun, and sisterhood. With more energy than anyone I've ever known, this diminutive dynamo showed a room of about 200 women how to thoroughly kick ass to protect themselves.

Letting women beat up on her for a living, Cindy shows the audience what to do, then has them gently practice on each other while yelling "NO," at the top of their lungs. It's a little intimidating, just being in the room.

At this event, Cindy had slides with inspirational messages cycling on big screens at the front of the room. The one that caught my attention the most said,

"You don't have to be nice to people who are trying to hurt you."

If I had taken her class when I was younger and had seen this message, I would have spared myself some trauma.

When I was a girl, we were taught to be "nice." I couldn't imagine slapping the face of a man who acted fresh. That would have been too "uncool." Unfortunately, my "coolness" got me into situations I couldn't get out of. If I hadn't been worried about being "nice," I wouldn't have bought into the narrative that made me feel like I had no choice in the situation. As an adult, I've learned to speak my voice, be an advocate for myself, and set boundaries. But what if I had known this earlier?

Cindy's mission, to teach women of all ages how to recognize and avoid dangerous situations and fight back when necessary, was inspired by a tragic event in her life. Her neighbor and best friend since the first grade was murdered in the basement of her college dorm the summer after their freshman year. On her website, Cindy says, "As young girls, Julie and I knew how to dance, swim and drive a car, but we didn't know how to protect our bodies in a dangerous situation. I now travel the country teaching women and young girls the lifesaving skills that Julie and I never had the opportunity to learn."

I've sat in on a couple of her classes now, and I can tell you that you'll leave the event feeling confident that you can easily scare off an attacker, if not seriously maim them.

Cindy's fierceness is contagious

We must teach women, young and old, to own their power when it comes to standing up for ourselves so our daughters, granddaughters, nieces, and friends won't become victims of violence. We pass our knowledge along from one generation of women to the next. For example, my mother taught me to be a strong, independent woman, and that is what I try to pass on to others through my actions and words.

As we continue to teach the women who follow us, our strength will grow exponentially through the generations.

Eventually, we may even reach a time where women won't have to live with the same fear, intimidation, and violence.

Recently I read an opinion piece by Mona Eltahawy, "What the world would look like if we taught girls to rage." In this article, she said that girls worldwide are taught that they are vulnerable or weak at a young age. Research in the article showed that by the time girls are 10 years old, they believe it.

We must find our inner strength to rage out about violence against women. These acts are about so much more than physical abuse. This vulnerability is one of the ways women are held back and not allowed to play. Instead of holding the criminal responsible, the victim gets the blame, with excuses about how it will ruin the rest of the attackers' lives. Never mind the impact the attackers' "indiscretion" will have on the rest of the survivors' lives. We can't expect someone else to always be around to come to our rescue. We have to learn how to scare off an attacker – and believe we can do it.

The truth is we don't want to think about these attacks because we want to believe that people are basically good and won't hurt us. Because we want to believe the best of people, we don't always pay attention to what's going on around us. The saddest truth is that from 1994 to 2010, statistics have steadily found that 78 percent of sexual violence involved an offender who was a family member, intimate partner, friend, or acquaintance. Strangers committed only about 22 percent of all sexual violence. These strangers frequently manipulate, intimidate, and confuse victims to get what they want and may seem like nice people. They're not.

While we've been taught that we are the weaker sex, it simply isn't true. (I pity the fool that would try to mess with me now!) We must be prepared to stand up for ourselves as fiercely as we would for someone else. Amazingly, putting up any kind of fight is usually enough to get an attacker to leave you alone. Defending ourselves isn't about who is the strongest. How successful a woman is at deflecting an attacker directly depends on her ability to have the confidence to fight back. This is what Cindy teaches so beautifully.

How can you turn your anger into power and harness that rage to fight for something you believe in?

Thriving Through Chaos

It is possible to bloom during chaos

I've given a lot of thought to what I want to write in response to the hearings around the appointment of Brett Kavanaugh to the Supreme Court and all the issues brought up in the political arena. I've experienced a whole gamut of emotions. I've been heartbroken, hurt, inflamed, disappointed, distressed, despondent – and tired.

This controversy weighs heavily on all of us. Have you noticed how tense and hostile it's feeling out in the world? People yell at each other in traffic, say hateful things, and call others names, with more scowls than smiles on faces. It's like the filter between social media, where people feel safe to be nasty, and the real world has evaporated. This animosity seems to add an extra feeling of hopelessness, making everything feel so much darker.

I don't know about you, but I'm tired of feeling all this tension and anger in my body. My shoulders are hiked up to my ears, my jaw muscles sore from clenching, and my stomach aches. Seriously, something has to give! It looks like what's got to change is my reaction to the stress. I'm not talking about being less passionate about what I believe or disconnecting from what's going on. In the Finishing School for Modern Women class "Embracing Change," we look for strategies to cope with change and thrive through it.

Take a pause and remember that anger is self-righteous.

In our "Turning Anger into Power" class at the Finishing School, we talk about how anger is moralistic. This emotion has everything to do with our values and the systems of ethics we're personally devoted to. Because of this, we feel justified in being angry when we're standing up for our beliefs. As a result, our existence turns into an Us versus Them scenario, with each side believing they're the ones on the side of good, so everyone who disagrees with them must be evil. But, of course, it's much more complicated than that.

So, even when I feel that I'm the one in the right, I will stop to ask myself if it is my responsibility to make sure everyone agrees and lives by my same system of ethics. Is my self-righteousness worth this particular relationship? Can we agree to disagree and have a civil conversation? After all, it's not that hard to find topics we share and can agree on.

Practice surrender.

Making myself sick with worry about what may happen in the future will not change the outcome. I can do what is within my power to impact the situation, and then I have to release it. My mantra for situations like this is, "Stay positive. Focus on the present. Keep moving forward." It reminds me of all the important stuff when trying to find my way through a tough situation. Surrendering isn't easy, but I'm learning to let go of what I can't control.

One thing that helps me let go is that I trust that I will be okay no matter what happens. I know this because I've seen what has happened in my life when the worst-case scenario did come true. As a result of these situations, the changes in my life were often the best thing that could have happened. Although it has been a struggle at times, my reinvented life was far better than before.

Work in meditation every day.

Stilling the mind and meditating is a great way to hit the reset button, especially when it all gets too overwhelming. Taking this time to focus is a huge help to my body and mind. It's also one of the secrets to learning how to surrender. Believe it or not, just not thinking about things for a while really can make the best answers clearer. It's no wonder that one of the steps of the recognized creative process is incubation. Like an incubator for premature babies in hospitals, giving your brain a rest gives your ideas extra time to develop and grow, consciously and subconsciously.

I like to use guided meditations with someone in a soothing voice, talking me through how to still my mind. Listening helps me focus, so I don't fall asleep or sit and worry. My new favorite is the "F*ck That" meditation. It won't be for you if you don't care for strong language, but it really works and is only three minutes long. It makes me laugh, and that's a good thing.

Laugh more.

Laughter is good for the soul, and during stressful times we can all use a good laugh. Laughing reduces stress hormones, adds joy to life, and strengthens relationships. Unfortunately, we don't laugh enough as adults, especially when under pressure. Watching and reading funny stuff, being around funny people, playing with my goofy dog, and trying not to take myself too seriously works for me.

Even smiling helps. I've been consciously working on having a resting smiley face, rather than a resting bitch face, simply by smiling when I think of it. I especially try to do this when I'm feeling impatient. It's calming, and often people react with a smile back.

When in doubt, act with love.

We need extra kindness right now. The past few weeks have been challenging. Reading everyone's stories about what the Kavanaugh Supreme Court hearings brought up for them has been heart-wrenching. There's a lot of anger, and fear, around these violent acts, and we all have a lot of healing to do. Coming together and talking about our experiences is how we work through the pain and shame because keeping it hidden only makes it worse. Love is more powerful than anger.

We need to be kinder to each other, even if we don't agree on everything. Our political affiliations don't mean that we are enemies. We are all humans. When we can't find a way to come together to work on our problems, we reach an impasse where we spend more time fighting with each other than making things better. I don't exactly know how to make this happen, but I know that we'll make more progress if we start listening to each other and having civil conversations about solutions rather than whom to blame.

I have been making a conscious effort to be nicer to people, especially helpers in service occupations. I have a feeling they're bearing the brunt of all this anger. Being kind and patient relieves my stress, and by the faces of these helpers,

I think it does theirs too. It's not that hard. It just takes a little empathy. We need to be kinder to ourselves too, and ask, "What do I need right now to take care of myself?"

Remember: Life is meant to be lived joyously.

Holding anger in our bodies for extended periods of time is exhausting. What will you do to diffuse anger to give yourself some peace every once in a while?

Chapter Five

Never Finish Advocating

How We Treat Our Sisters

Working Together

When I was in Chicago over the 2018 holidays, my mother told me that there wouldn't be a Women's March in 2019 in the Windy City. The organizers called it off, giving the official reason that they had already spent their energy and resources on a mid-term "March to the Polls" voting push. However, there's a lot of speculation and controversy about other reasons for the cancellation.

I also read about a march in California canceled due to the lack of participation of women of color. This issue is just the tip of the iceberg of more significant matters around the fight for equality.

The cancellation of these events makes me sad for a couple of reasons. Coming together, as women and allies, to publicly stand up and stand together to say "no more" and fight for equality for all of us is what the Women's March symbolizes to me. We show the world that we're willing to fight for our rights by showing up. But, I understand this is a complicated issue.

Women of diverse backgrounds are fighting for issues from an entirely different kind of reality than I live with. Looking at the wage gap of what women make compared to men makes this painfully obvious. Did you know that while white women earn 81.3% of what men make, it's much worse for Black women (68%) and even worse for Hispanic women (62.2%), and worst of all for Native American women (51%)? While this is painfully wrong and must be addressed, these and many issues we all share would be better served by learning to listen to each other and work together as allies, not enemies. Canceling events because people aren't willing to work it out is disappointing.

Speaking my truth

I spoke at the Women's March in my hometown in 2018, and this year I've been honored to serve on the committee to select speakers. I am excited that we have incredible speakers and entertainers lined up and that we achieved our goal of inclusivity to look at the complicated issues of equality.

What canceling marches says about women working together also makes me sad. When I hear women talk about how hard it is to work with other women, it makes my heart hurt. In business, people are often pitted against each other to "get ahead," and some women take this very seriously. As a result, insecurities, fears, and other emotions get stirred up, and our worst tendencies emerge.

Competition is a patriarchal value that women don't have to ascribe to. Instead, we need to learn the matriarchal value of collaboration, focus on the vision, and learn to come together. Letting these values divide us has beaten down our efforts every single time. Now is not the time to pull apart – this is a time to unify.

When we can't unify, it costs us. It cost us the Equal Rights Amendment (ERA). This simple statement which says, "Equality of rights under the law shall not be denied or abridged by the United States or by any State on account of sex," would have constitutionally protected the rights of women – and men. Imagine how much further along we'd be If women had been able to come together in the 1970s to address tremendous issues, like breaking down the barriers women face in being able to support themselves and their families.

Sadly, the ERA still hasn't been added as the 28th amendment to the Constitution. When the law passed in 1972, the legislation included a seven-year deadline to get 38 states to ratify the amendment. Congress extended the deadline to 1982, but ERA opponents divided women and were able to stall the momentum. Only three states needed to make this important amendment the law when the time expired.

Although the 38th state finally ratified the amendment in 2020, Congress must eliminate the previous deadline to make it part of the Constitution, protect current laws, and preserve gender equality in the U.S. Constitution. Call your senators and representatives and let them know it's time to get this done!

We must recognize that we're never going to agree on everything – and understand that unity is not uniformity. No one said working together was going to be easy. One of the traits that women who make things happen have in common is their feistiness.

I've spent a lifetime working with these spirited women, starting with my own mother, and believe I have achieved feisty status. We are strong, opinionated, stubborn, mouthy broads who aren't afraid to go toe-to-toe to fight for what we believe. There are going to be clashes. That's okay. Sometimes we'll have to go with the consensus. But when we don't get our way, we should try to stay, support, and contribute to the greater good and not get bogged down in the minutia that won't matter in the long run. Of course, there are exceptions when the situation is toxic or won't improve. The Joy Suck Rule overrides everything.

Something else these women who make things happen have in common is their passion for excellence, which I find inspiring. Part of what I love about being a member of the National Federation of Press Women, my girl gang, the Heifers, and being chair of the Friends of the Wichita Art Museum has been the formidable women I've gotten to know and work with. I've learned a lot about working on these committees. I hope my tips will help your collaboration efforts for the greater good.

Speak your truth with respect.

With this crowd, you've gotta be bold and ready to speak up to make your viewpoint known. Chances are no one will specifically ask you what you think, so be assertive enough to put it out there when you have something important to say. The more concise you are, the more you'll be listened to, so stick to key discussion points.

Don't make it personal.

How information is given and received is important, so don't make or take things personally. Personal attacks obviously don't work in collaborations. Don't go there. Probably too often, we read something into conversations and feel attacked, which may or may not be the intention. Whatever the truth is, it's always better to let that stuff go. After all, being free of both praise and criticism, not caring what others' opinions are of you, is one of the secrets to happiness.

Listen with love while others speak.

One of the kindest, most respectful things we do for others is to truly listen to them. Not just think about what we're going to say next. I believe what people want most is to be heard. When people don't feel they're being listened to, emotions get extreme. So listen with an open mind by suspending judgment or making decisions until the discussion ends.

Pick your battles.

I've found that when conversations get argumentative, I have to decide how important that fight is to me. Some people will argue just for the sake of arguing. Usually, it's more important for that person to feel they're "right," leading to time-wasting conversations over semantics and what-ifs on issues they may not even care about. Fight for what you feel strongly about and let the rest go.

Keep your eye on the vision.

The most important aspect of taking action is to keep moving closer to your goals. YOUR goals, not someone else's. When you know where you're headed, you can't afford to let yourself get distracted by what other people are doing or think you should be doing. Decide your direction and how you'll move through the world. We join organizations and collaborate for a purpose, which becomes your vision for community work. Focusing on what you hope will be achieved through your actions is the best work we can do.

We are stronger when we work together!

What strategies can you put into place to improve how you work and play with others?

Conversations of Color

Some of the most impactful experiences of my life have come from fierce conversations. That has certainly been the case at the Conversations of Color panel discussions I've hosted at the Finishing School for Modern Women.

I've moderated inclusive panels of women who agreed to talk candidly about their experiences around race relations and what we can do to support each other. A big thank you to everyone on the panels and in the audience for being vulnerable enough to join in. Although there were many backgrounds and ideological differences between us, everyone kept an open mind. The conversation was respectful, profoundly honest, and eye-opening. Here are a few of my takeaways.

It takes more than love.

While there's a lot of talk about love triumphing over hate, love is complicated. It's easy to love the people we agree with, but what about people with different viewpoints? Love doesn't look the same for everyone. For some people, love must be earned. Because my fundamental nature is to love people, I try to accept people for who they are as an individual. I love most people automatically – unless the person's actions change my mind.

During the panel discussion, the idea was brought up that respect for our fellow humans is more important than love in how we treat each other. I'm still mulling that over. For me, respect is something that's earned. However, I think giving people the benefit of the doubt shows respect for human dignity, and that value is a vital part of human rights.

Treating someone with dignity means asking for and listening to their concerns. This includes people who will be impacted by conversations and decisions while respecting their right to make their own choices. Dignity is our inherent value and worth as human beings; everyone is born with it.

We all want to be treated as valuable. This shared desire for dignity transcends all our differences, putting our human identity above everything else. The need to be seen, heard, listened to, and treated fairly is the glue that holds our relationships together. To be recognized, understood, and to feel safe in the world gives our lives hope and possibility.

The Queen and Me

Words have power.

Perpetuating stereotypes is so ingrained that we may not even realize we're doing it. That certainly happened to me at one of the panel discussions. It is my biggest takeaway and my biggest regret.

I have always thought the label "angry Black women" is ridiculous. If my DNA were different, I'd be the angriest Black woman you've ever met. The way the systems are stacked against these women, including pay and primary medical care, would be enough to make anyone furious. So when I met Queen Mary Dean, and she introduced herself to me as an angry Black woman, I connected with her immediately.

I love people who are unafraid and unapologetic to show the world their true, authentic self – and Mary is living that. For example, when asked how she refers to herself regarding race, Mary's answer "Black Queen" is so meaningful to her that she has it tattooed on her leg. I hold the story of meeting Mary close to heart for her authenticity, but I don't think of her as angry.

I enjoyed working with Mary on lining up speakers for the Women's March, so I said "yes" when she asked me to be on a panel about race relations and mental health for her organization Black Women Empowered. Later, she let me use the idea of that panel and agreed to participate in the "Activate: Conversations of Color" panel discussion at the Finishing School. I have a lot of respect for Mary, love working with her, and will continue to look for ways for us to collaborate. Would I do this if I thought of her as an angry, unreasonable, hostile person? Of course not.

When I introduced Mary for the panel, I made the mistake of telling everyone the story of when we met. Because the phrase "angry Black woman" means something entirely different to me, I didn't realize the power of those words. I didn't recognize how it might affect the way the people watching the panel saw her and how we've unconsciously been taught to think about women who won't back down their passion when it comes to injustice. Since this is one of the ways women are held back, I feel horrible for attaching that label to someone I admire so much.

I've apologized to Mary for my ignorance, and of course, she has given me eternal grace. She says she's comfortable owning that title. Nevertheless, her introduction was a powerful lesson for me. Fortunately, passion and compassion are closely related, and Mary is fluent in both languages.

Sometimes the best thing to do is listen.

I am always amazed at the insights we get when we simply stop and listen. Our society is so fragmented it seems like we're living in different realities. People are dividing into a "us" vs. "them" mentality, making the "them" less than human so we can justify our viewpoint. But, if we took the time to sit down and talk, we'd find that we're much more alike than different, especially when it comes to what we need to survive and thrive.

While we didn't come up with any earth-shattering solutions for how we can support each other, I think that just talking about these issues gave us more insights into what it's like to walk a mile in someone else's shoes. Learning to listen is a fantastic start.

Make the world a better place where you are.

What can you do to show more support for our sisters?

Discoveries

One of my favorite things about being Headmistress of the Finishing School for Modern Women is bringing people together to talk about what's going on in the world. Not to commiserate as much as to strategize. As a community of Modern Women, we can make an impact by coming up with solutions and talking about how we can help each other.

Women have a unique way of looking at situations that differs from men. Maybe it's the gift we've been given to grow humans inside our bodies. Perhaps it's an "outsider" perspective forced on us from being told to watch silently from the sideline. We certainly understand what abuse feels like since most of us have experienced some form of that in silent secrecy.

Women have been socialized to be the caregivers in society. It hurts us when we see blatant abuse. We often won't fight for ourselves but threaten those we love, and our inner warrior queen will come out to slay.

At a time when people have had to take it to the streets to take a stand that black lives matter, there are many battles to fight and wrongs to be righted. It is time to expand our worldview to see beyond our experience and learn from others. Our recent "Activate!" Advocacy Training panel discussion was a fantastic experience. Here's what I learned.

Not being racist isn't enough.

It is time to take a stand for antiracism. The difference is subtle but powerful. Antiracism is about actively opposing racism to promote change and racial equality. Read about what you can do to examine your own bias.

This panel of activists that aren't shy
about sharing their passion

Show up.

The simplest thing we can do to be an ally is show up. In other words, to take action. There are a lot of ways to stand up besides protesting. Donating money and/or time to nonprofits that benefit the Black community, spending money with Black-owned businesses, or attending events where you may be the only white person are a few suggestions. These easy actions will also help broaden the diversity of your friends, contacts, and allies.

Raise antiracist children.

Changing society by raising children who can identify racism and stand up against it is part of the revolution too. So don't forget it or think what you're doing as a parent is insignificant.

Keep your hands to yourself.

I'm shocked that I even have to say this. DO NOT ask to touch a Black woman's hair, and most especially, DO NOT touch her hair without asking. You'll pull away with a nub – and you deserve to. I mean, really. I can tell you from experience that taming textured hair is an art form. My hair can go from fabulous to frizz just by sweeping the hair away from my eyes. If you're curious and can't stand it, go to a wig shop and ask the people working there all the questions you want. You might even be allowed to touch the wigs.

Be a sponsor.

Sometimes as allies, we need to walk beside our sisters of color. Other times we need to walk in front and break down barriers. Watch for opportunities to connect and recommend Black and brown women into what you're doing. Be purposely inclusive in the places where you have the power to be.

Don't be afraid to ask.

We may worry too much about being offensive when inviting people of color into our circles. We want to be more inclusive, but we worry about making someone feel "token." This fear keeps us segregated. Instead, reach out to your friends and contacts and ask for recommendations. Ask people you know to invite friends and broaden your connections. People feel like they belong in places where there are people who look like them, so don't stop at asking one person.

Get Curious.

One of the things I hear most from Black women is that they are tired of trying to teach people what it means to be Black in this society. It is exasperating how long they've been trying to inform, mostly to people who will not listen. There are many books you can read or listen to. There are podcasts and all kinds of amazing information waiting for you on the internet. Google it!

Not everyone agrees.

The part of the discussion that got the most passionate was about what needs to be done about policing. Law enforcement is a sticky, complicated issue that's emotionally charged because it keys into our most basic human needs – safety. That Black parents must have "The Talk" with their children about surviving police interaction is a huge red flag that change needs to happen. I don't think anyone has all the answers for police reform yet, but lots of dialogue with citizen input around this topic is past due.

Get comfortable with being uncomfortable.

People are complicated, and so are the issues around us. Learning more about what's going on in the world can feel like wearing a hair suit. There is so much anger and animosity toward people who hold different opinions than us, and our society is seriously divided. That should make us all feel uncomfortable.

Don't get invested.

Learning about the injustices in the world will bring up powerful emotions. Don't get invested in those reactions. Experience them, then let them go. It's part of growth and learning to process anger, shame, conflict, righteous indignation, guilt, and all the feels. help you go deeper.

We all need to expand our worldview and realize that not everyone's experience is the same as ours and love them anyway. Or at least get to know someone before judging them.

What will you do to step out of your social bubble to expand your outlook on the world?

Showing my PRIDE

I've never wanted to be like everyone else. Maybe that's because I've been blessed with naturally red hair. Whether you want it or not, having red hair makes you stand out. From the time I was a little girl, my family told me I was special because of my hair color. I believed them.

But part of not wanting to be like everyone else means you don't exactly fit in. That can be tough on us square pegs. It can leave us feeling isolated. People who are afraid or angry about people who don't "go along with the program" can be cruel. I can't begin to tell you how much I was teased just for having red hair. Unmercifully. Since I was proud of being "special," their words didn't faze me. I knew they were just jealous of my boogie.

Being the social butterfly that I am, isolation doesn't work for me. So, I started looking around in the corners. By that, I mean paying attention to the people that socially mill around the periphery. In the "Making Connections that Count" class at the Finishing School for Modern Women, I give the advice that, if you're shy or introverted, look around the corners and in the kitchen for the people who feel as awkward as you. They're usually just as nervous about fitting in as you are.

Special bonus: These are often the most interesting people in the room, with thought-provoking perspectives gained by being observant. The corners are a great place to find new friends for us square pegs.

Unknowingly, this is what I did in high school. I started looking for new friends in the corners. I explored other areas rather than longing to be one of the "popular," beautiful people where I knew I didn't fit in. That's where I found my people –

the creatives. I connected with the thespians, artists, literati, and musicians. What a magical world!

Thanks to my family upbringing, I already loved everything creative and fit in like I'd found home. Finding the exciting world of the glitterati made me care even less about conforming to a cookie-cutter world. I actively avoided fitting in and decided always to let my freak flag fly!

Being with my new friends expanded my consciousness and helped me see life differently – the beauty, splendor, and ugly realities. People become outsiders for lots of reasons. I'd like to think it was my conscious choice to be there. Other people are outsiders because they don't follow societal norms, especially when it comes to who they want to pair up with. In the late 70s, when I was in high school, sexual preference was a stigma that went beyond getting ostracized. It got them killed. Being gay and "out" was a huge risk.

I had never been around anyone who admitted to being gay at that point in my life. Sadly, I knew boys that picked on kids for "being a fag." When I was around those boys, I laughed at their jokes, making fun of limp-wristed caricatures. But then, I made a new friend who changed my life and how I view the world forever.

When we met, we recognized the spark we saw in each other. The spiritual connection was instantaneous. We started spending a lot of time together, never running out of things to talk about and explore and having way too much fun doing it – much to his mother's chagrin. (I still think she thinks I'm a bad influence.)

It wasn't long into our friendship that Kevin came out to me and told me he is gay. We had a long conversation, and I asked him every question I could think of to try and understand why he would make that choice. It seemed like such a drastic thing to do.

From this conversation, I started to understand that this was not a conscious choice. Kevin knew who he was and was not attracted to, the same way I did – he just knew. To pretend otherwise wasn't an option.

I thought about our friendship, deciding whether or not I wanted to continue it, considering this discovery. Publicly being friends with someone gay instantly makes you an ally, whether that's your intention or not. There is a risk to that. Being friends with someone gay means you love them and accept them just as they are, even if that isn't your preference. It didn't take me long to decide that it was too late. The decision had already been made. I loved Kevin, and it didn't matter to me who else he loved.

This is what love looks like

I am happy to say that we're celebrating 40 years of friendship this year. We stayed close even during a sixteen-year long-distance relationship when Kevin moved to New York not long after we graduated from high school. He moved back several years ago, and we've picked up right where we left off – much to his mother's chagrin.

So much more than a brother, Kevin is my heart and soul, and I am grateful and fortunate to have such a close, loyal friend. He's seen me through two husbands and countless boyfriends, and I know this man will be in my life forever. I have never regretted my decision.

The 1980s were a hard time to be gay and to have friends that are gay. The AIDS crisis was like a massacre, watching so many talented, vibrant young men waste away just as they were beginning to contribute what would have been amazing work. My creative circle was hit hard, and I lost a heart-wrenching number of friends. Every time I see the AIDS Memorial Quilt, it feels like a family reunion, no matter what city I'm in. I wonder what my friends that passed would be doing today. I wonder what other mind-blowing music Freddy Mercury would have given us.

The Stonewall riots had happened about 10 years earlier, and more brave men and women were choosing to show their true rainbow colors. Then AIDS hit – and things changed. At that time, people were ignorant and afraid they would catch the disease just by being around someone gay.

From this fear, people who are gay were ostracized and demonized more than ever before, being told this disease was their punishment from God. Because of this cruel false judgment, little was done to find a cure or even offer relief to people with this tragic illness. We watched our friends turn into skeletons right before our eyes while more people showed the signs of the disease. We knew it was really hate that was killing them.

Being an ally became even more important to me during the AIDs crisis, never believing for one minute that God could be as cruel as mortals. Standing up and helping bring awareness about what was going on and getting help for people in our community was important to me.

I volunteered on the board of ArtAID for 20 years, working with artists, stylists, designers, entertainers, and so many other creatives to put on this annual event that combined art, fashion, music, and theater. We helped raise over $1.5 million to give people in our community living with HIV and AIDS the support they needed with daily living expenses, housing, and food. There have been medical breakthroughs since that help people manage the disease, so it isn't quite the death sentence it once was. However, I still think it's too important a health risk to ignore.

I continue to be an ally to my LGBTQ+ brothers and sisters and feel strongly that love is love and that love is divine. This June, for PRIDE month, I planned to start writing an allies column for Liberty Press, the longest-running LGBTQ publication in Kansas. Unfortunately, my friend and editor of the publication, Kristi Parker, had a stroke and became one with the universe earlier this year and the publication folded.

One of the best things Kristi did was help young people realize they weren't alone. As a journalist, she saved many lives by being brave enough to put the conversation into print. She let the square pegs and outsiders know that it really does get better, that their people are waiting for them. I am sad I can't be a part of that.

While I won't be writing a monthly article about my ally PRIDE for Liberty Press, I remember and honor Kristi and all my friends whose lives ended too soon.

How can you be an ally to someone you love?

Will We Know?

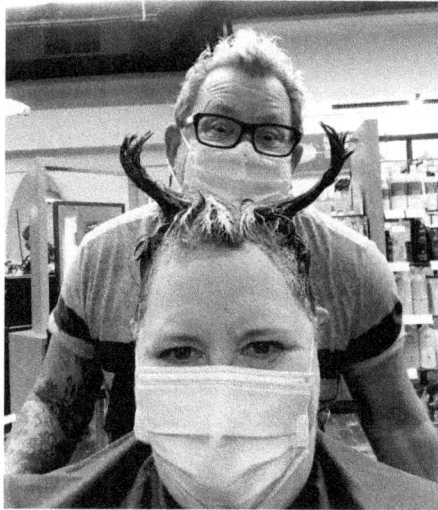

My first hairdo after the pandemic
lockdown

Since the COVID pandemic has turned more of us into introverts, I wonder if we'll have any idea how to act when we feel more comfortable seeing each other in person. According to one of the college students in the class I'm teaching online at Wichita State University this semester, we've already forgotten. She works at a restaurant and has noticed that people have already lost many of the social graces we all take for granted.

For us social butterflies, isolation has been tough. I'll probably act like an over-eager puppy the first chance I get to see a bunch of people at once. Meanwhile, all the natural introverts I know have been relieved. They're happy there's no pressure to attend events in person. It's going to be the hardest for them to make public appearances in the future. Even though I love meeting new people and can talk to anyone, I have a feeling I'll feel a bit awkward at first, too.

If the thought of networking makes you feel queasy, you're not alone. In the "Making Connections that Count" class we offer at the Finishing School for Modern Women, I've learned that people are worried about many things when meeting new people. They don't know how to get conversations started and are afraid they won't be interesting.

However, the biggest reason people are uncomfortable about networking is that they're worried about being ignored, or worse, rejected. This fear takes us right back to when we weren't invited to play schoolyard games and that little person inside us who remembers what it feels like to be awkward around people we don't know.

Even if networking isn't your favorite brand of disco, you can find a way to work around the discomfort. It takes creativity, but you can do it your way. Here are some tips for reluctant networkers and those who need a reminder.

Find your style.

Discover what works for you. If you're more outgoing, look for big groups of people to join. If you're more reserved, you can find someone else in the room who seems reserved and meet them. They're usually the most interesting people in the room anyway.

Have a goal of what you want to accomplish – an agenda.

What help do you need? What are you looking for? How many new people do you want to meet? Make it fun. Think of it as a scavenger hunt.

Make sure you use your powers for good and not evil.

The goal can't be for purely selfish reasons. People can see right through egotistical intentions. Remember, to have friends, we must be a friend.

Arrive a little early. You can be the welcoming committee.

Be the first to meet the movers and shakers that organized the event, and then as people come in, you can welcome them. See, you already fit in!

Learn by watching others.

Look for people who look at ease working a room. Notice what that person does and add what you like to your style.

Bring a friend.

Invite a friend to go with you. If you're more introverted, ask a more extroverted friend who knows a lot of people to go with you. Work out a plan for introductions.

Meet a friend.

If you're going to a big party, find out who will be there before you go, so you know you have someone comfortable to hang out with.

Get in the mood.

Do things before the party that build your confidence: breathe, strike the Wonder Woman pose, or listen to songs that pump you up.

Remember the "So What" factor.

What's the worst thing that could happen? What's so bad about being rejected by someone you don't even know? If you're not having fun, you can always leave. I know it's time for me to go when I start feeling like I'm waiting for a bus.

I'm excited to see society reopen, whenever that happens. I've been feeling a bit pent up, and it will do my heart some good to get out of the house. I miss our community very much. Besides, I'm looking forward to a reason to get dressed and made-up.

How will you use these tips to up your networking game?

Gratitude in Action

While I was thinking about ways we can actively work to build self-confidence. I had asked my friends on Facebook for ideas. They shared their fabulous suggestions. Now, weeks later, there is one response that sticks to my brain like gum on a shoe: Perform an act of kindness.

The idea of feeling good by doing something good isn't terribly surprising. But that was just a piece of my friend's response. She told me she's grateful for what she has in her life and likes to perform acts of kindness to share the love. My brain's immediate response was, "Well, that's gratitude in action!" And that's where I'm stuck.

Around the end of November, we talk a lot about being grateful. I don't think about the story of the pilgrims at Thanksgiving at all. Instead, I look at this holiday as a time to recognize abundance and be grateful for what I've received. Now that I've got the idea of "gratitude in action" caught in my head, being thankful somehow doesn't seem enough.

I'm grateful for this guy

Not that many years ago, I decided to focus my attention on relationships that are equal parts give and take. I realized that

I had done most of the giving for too long, and when I needed a little something in return, I was ghosted.

Part of my problem in giving too much is that I'm still learning to ask for and accept help. I own that. But moving forward, the relationships I'm going to put my energy into are ones that I don't have to ask. They're already there, offering support before I know I need it. So I try to do the same in return.

I've asked myself, "How is being grateful any different than a friend that's all take and no give?" "What does 'Gratitude in action' mean to me?" I love my life, and I am grateful for all the gifts I'm given every day. How do I reflect that? How do I give back in my relationship with the Divine, to give more than lip service to what is in my heart?

This time, rather than crowdsourcing the answer, I pressed my friends for answers in live conversations. You probably know me well enough by now to know I have a list of solutions for you. I do love a plan.

Acknowledge strangers.

Sometimes it's a kind word or even a smile that can give you a little lift when you need it. Looking someone you don't know in the eye, smiling at them, and saying hello is an easy way to say, "Stranger, I see you."

Recently I was listening to an interview on NPR with Brene Brown about our relationships with people. She talked about how we are all connected yet growing apart from each other in these divisive times. We need to be more human, and acknowledging strangers is an excellent place to start.

Practice courtesy.

I can't say "common courtesy" because it isn't so common. When I say "thank you" and "please" to helpers in stores and drive-throughs, they always act surprised. We all know what to do. It's not that hard. It is opening the door for someone or letting a person with fewer items in their cart cut in front of you in line at the grocery store. These little gestures make the world a much better place.

During the holidays is a perfect time to practice this skill. This time of year is the absolute worse for how people in the retail and hospitality industries are treated. People act like their agenda is the only one that counts, and everyone else better stay out of their way.

I try to be extra kind to these low-paid, hard workers who are on their feet most of the day. I carry gold stars in my purse to give away in recognition of exceptional service or having a sunny disposition even when people are rude. I need a "Congrats for not killing anyone today" sticker too.

Show and tell.

If you're grateful and you know it, say thank you. Showing appreciation was the number one answer in my unofficial "showing gratitude" poll of friends. Of course, saying the words is essential, but showing your appreciation in creative ways is what speaks the loudest. A hand-written thank-you note takes a few minutes to write and will last a lifetime in peoples' hearts, and probably in their filing cabinet too.

I've said "thank you" with pans of lasagna made from scratch, homemade chocolate chip cookies, and other goodies. The service of creating something in appreciation is meaningful to me. Maybe cooking isn't your jam, but maybe arts and crafts are your brand of disco. Whatever comes from your heart and comes out through your hands is a powerful way to say thanks.

One of the best ways to show businesses you appreciate them is through referrals. If you're happy doing business with someone, tell people about it, and help them spread the word. Share their newsletters. Write positive reviews about them online. "Like," comment, and share their posts on social media.

You can't imagine how much it helps businesses when people do this! I certainly appreciate it when people do this for me. (Was that too subtle?)

Be a daymaker.

When I worked for Aveda, I met David Wagner, the inspirational leader and founder of JUUT Salonspas in Minneapolis. After a profound life-saving experience with one of his regular clients, David recognized the impact that he has – that we all have – in making the world a better place, one person at a time. It changed his life, and mine too.

He wrote "Life as a Daymaker: How to Change the World by Making Someone's Day." Then, he started the Daymaker Movement to spread the idea and create more Daymakers, "person who performs intentional acts of kindness with the intention of making the world a better place." That's how I've tried to live my life since I met David.

Acts of kindness.

Do something kind for someone for no reason at all. Send a text to someone on your mind just to let that person know you're thinking about them. Give credit where credit is due, especially when you get a compliment for the work someone else did. Look at the world with fresh eyes to see what is truly going on around you and acknowledge that the people you encounter are in pain and hungry for kindness. We all are. It is what makes us human.

This year while stuffing myself with turkey and bourbon sweet potatoes in the company of some of the people I love most in this world, I will thank the Divine for all my blessings. In the spirit of gratitude in action, I will be more mindful of how I reflect appreciation.

How will you turn your gratitude into action?

Try a Little Tenderness

You never know how your actions will impact others. The words you say. The expression on your face. Even just giving someone a smile, for no reason at all, can make a difference in someone's day.

I have found this to be true many times in my life, on both the giving and receiving end. I've discovered that, what seems like a little, often forgotten, thing to me has deeply impacted someone else. For example, at the beginning of June, I started posting what I think of as "You are" daily affirmations on my personal Facebook feed. I started with the post, "You are mighty!" I've heard from friends, online and in-person, how much these posts mean to them and what a bright spot it's been in their feed and day.

When the college class I teach was getting ready to start in August, and I knew my life was about to get much busier, I warned my friends that I was planning to end the affirmations. The response I got was overwhelming! People called, messaged, and tracked me down in person to let me know how upset they were that I was planning to stop the posts. They begged me to continue. How could I say "no" to that? I must continue – for a while longer.

Years ago, I heard a story about a woman in the city where I live who decided she couldn't go on and planned to take her own life. As she was walking downtown, a woman walked past her, made eye contact, smiled, and said "hello." That smile and recognition were what the woman credited with changing her mind, deciding to stick around.

Searching for the article online just now, I found that this story isn't as rare as one would think. I discovered many stories about how a simple smile took a person from feeling invisible and unworthy to help them feel noticed and alive. A friendly gesture made the difference between life and death. Now, I'm not saying suicide prevention is that easy, but why not smile at people anyway? You never know what it will do.

With all the natural disasters we've had lately, the silver lining has been the stories of how people have selflessly aided others. Recognized as "heroes," these people often say they were doing what anyone would do. But is this true? In Elizabeth Svoboda's study "The Surprising Science of Selflessness," a case is made that we "all have the capacity to rise to the occasion when disaster strikes," with evidence that we can all become more compassionate. Many studies have shown our brains light up in the same areas we use to process pleasure and rewards when we give to charities. It feels good to help others.

Interestingly, our brain is hardwired to be kind. Darwin believed that sympathy is the strongest instinct we have. We often see that demonstrated in times of crisis, when people put their desire to help others before their self-interests, sometimes even risking their lives to save someone they've never met. This risky behavior is more likely to happen if we've been through hard times ourselves. We are more likely to help others in the same situation when we have lived through suffering. Our empathy for others grows as we gain more understanding of how tough the circumstances can be because we've lived through them ourselves. So see, your suffering isn't in vain!

Being kind not only makes you feel good, but it's also good for you! Acts of kindness reduce heart disease, slow aging, and improve relationships. Have you ever noticed that older people who appear happy often look younger? It shows on their face. Kindness also has the power to heal. Research shows that human connection has the power to decrease pain, lessen anxiety, lower blood pressure, and increase the capacity of our immune system to fight disease. There are so many reasons to be kind. So why do we have to wait until a crisis to think and act kindly toward others?

When we can't seem to agree on anything, can we agree on kindness? You can make the decision to treat everyone, even those you disagree with, with more compassion. It's really pretty simple. Kindness is contagious. Spread some around!

What are you doing to bring up the kindness quotient?

A Gold Star for You!

Remember when you were a kid, what a thrill it was to find a shiny gold star on your school paper? Of course, not all teachers give gold stars, so some people may never have experienced this exact feeling of glittery, giddy accomplishment. That's a shame. I have been known to give the college students in the Entrepreneurship in the Arts class I teach at Wichita State University gold stars on their papers when they've done an extra good job. They may find this eccentric, but there's something magical about this symbol of achievement that takes us back to our childhood.

I love to give out gold stars. I carry these golden prizes in my wallet and hand them out when the opportunity presents itself. I started handing them out when I began writing "please ask for ID" on the signature line of my debit and credit cards as an extra security precaution. Unfortunately, I found that very few people even look at the signatures on the cards, let alone compare them to the signature on the receipt. It felt like such a momentous occasion when someone was actually paying attention that I decided to surprise them with a gold star sticker.

My favorite part of giving gold stars is the reaction I get from people. I thank the person for doing a great job, tell them they've earned a gold star and why. The look of joy on their faces is priceless. Lots of people laugh. Some people have shed tears. But it always turns a frown upside down, on even the crankiest cuss. For example, at the Iditarod Trail Headquarters gift shop in Wasilla, Alaska, the gold star I gave one person created such a stir and made the rest of the staff so jealous I ended up giving everyone gold stars!

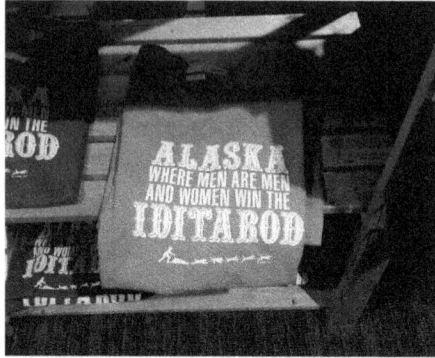

Gold stars for everyone!

We're all just big, grown-up kids pretending to be adults. Going back and tapping into the joy we felt when we were children is profound. Recently, professional musician and bully prevention activist Jenny Wood was a guest speaker for my college class. She inspired us all with what she shared about the music business. But, what I loved the most was what she said about having the confidence to get up on stage and own it like a rock star.

She said that she remembers what it felt like when she was a wee one and sang and danced in front of the mirror in her bedroom with complete abandon, just for the joy of it. When she performs, she goes back to that feeling, letting the pleasure of making music overcome all fears and self-doubt. She is my heroine.

Now I look for other reasons to give gold stars: excellent customer service, catching someone doing something nice for someone, or just because it seems like someone needs one. Now, more than ever, it looks like people are looking for reasons to be disgruntled.

It must be human nature to look for the bad in life instead of the good. So, let's try to focus on being just as free with our compliments as we are with our complaints. Telling people they're doing a great job is so easy to do and makes a big impact on their day. And I'll let you in on a little secret: It will brighten your day too.

I've noticed that it can be shocking to people to be complimented. I love telling complete strangers that they "look fabulous!" or that I appreciate something they've done. Some people look at me like I have three heads, but that's okay. There are people who don't know how to take a compliment or are suspicious about what I might be up to. With others, it's started conversations that have led to friendships. Acknowledging people, and showing that we see who they are, is one of the kindest acts we can do for one another. We all just want to be heard.

After all, it's the little things in life that make significant differences. A kind word. A friendly smile. A moment shared – a gold star sticker.

Who will you give a gold star to today?

Chapter Six

Never Finish Collaborating

How We Work Together

The Gift of Collaboration

When I started planning the Finishing School for Modern Women, I knew I would need help to achieve my mission. I want to help women gain the skills to claim their power and live happier, more successful lives, and I can't do that by myself. So from the beginning, I knew collaborating with people who had expertise in other areas would give our students more power through the knowledge that came from the community and shared experiences. Besides, it's hard to come up with all the ideas on my own, and I wouldn't want to even if I could.

Collaboration inspires me.

When things click with a creative partner, energy builds, and everything flows smoothly with brilliant ideas coming from seemingly nowhere. It's exciting to see where the class flows when someone else is involved, often in a completely different direction than I envisioned. I love it when the conversation gives me goosebumps, which has long been one of my body's ways to let me know when an idea is fantastic.

Collaboration helps me broaden my worldview.

Genuinely listening to others' ideas and points of view has helped me gain more empathy and understanding. For example, since I've chosen not to be a parent, I don't have any firsthand knowledge of what it must feel like to raise children. Collaborating with Dr. Natalie Grant on the "Parenting in the 21st Century" class helped me understand the reality of "mommy guilt." She also taught me about the strengths-based perspective of parenting, which nurtures natural strengths instead of thinking we must be good at everything. Looking at life through the lens of building strengths has helped me personally and professionally, long outliving the collaborative experience.

Collaboration is challenging.

Being good at working with others demands excellence in communication, relationship-building, and other unglamorous management techniques. It takes leaving your ego at the door and realizing that your ideas aren't the only good ones. Listening and learning from each other to make the outcome stronger is the sole object of the game. Taking in others' points of view doesn't make your ideas weaker or make you less in any way. On the contrary, building ideas together makes everyone stronger. It takes a great deal of respect for others and their opinions, and for yourself and the expertise and strengths, you bring to the relationship.

Of course, not all collaborations work out well. It's hard to listen to other opinions that may not be as elegant as ours. Over the past four years, most of my experiences have been good, but some have been real doozies. Not everyone is good at collaboration, and sometimes partnerships just don't click. It doesn't mean anyone was bad or did anything wrong, it just means we weren't a good fit. From these painful experiences, I've learned how important it is to be adaptive to differences in personalities and how to foster better cooperative relationships.

Pick your partners wisely.

Before even getting started in any partnership, it's important to get to know each other first. It's infinitely easier to work on projects with people you like and respect. It's worth taking some time to build a relationship before even deciding to work together. It's important to know if your philosophies are in alignment and if you can agree on the outcome and priorities of the project before you commit to working together.

I have to know our hearts are in the same place. I look for partners who have unheard voices and are unsung heroes, humbly working to strengthen our community. I like working with people who give credit where credit is due, recognizing the people who helped get them there, and being more concerned about making the world a better place than how it will benefit them personally.

Define the relationship.

Before getting started, take some time to define the relationship. Reach an agreement on how you'll work together, how you'll communicate and share files, your goals, and who will be in charge of what. It's also a good idea to create and communicate some boundaries around what you can and can't be flexible about. For example, boundaries could be around how much time to spend on the project, how long the project will last, or what you are and aren't willing to do. Don't just give these roles lip service. Putting it in writing so everyone knows what is expected will avoid a lot of heartaches later. The effort is worth every minute.

Communication is key.

So many of the problems people have with each other could be solved through improved communications, especially when we agree on how the relationship will work in advance. Still, feelings can get unintentionally hurt, people don't always stay in their lane, and sometimes life changes happen. Just talk about it!

Since we learned most of our coping skills when we were children, it's always important to remember that we're all still children in our heads. So shaming and being critical of others – and ourselves – is not constructive.

Be accountable.

Always do what you say you're going to do. There's nothing worse than breaking that agreement. Sure, it happens to everyone that we get overcommitted, and some plates crash to the floor, but if it happens too often, that's the reputation you get. Keep communication open. If you're not going to make a deadline, let the group know in advance. Send up a flare – ask for help — there's nothing wrong with that.

Be aware of what could go sideways.

Teaching at a university and being involved in volunteer organizations has taught me how group projects get sabotaged, usually by people with the best intentions. Some people will pick up the slack for everyone else, maybe because they think they're the only ones who can do things right, so they take on too many tasks. Sometimes they resent having to do everything or being unable to complete everything they've agreed to do.

Happy that someone has agreed to do too much, other people contribute little more than advice or criticism, constructive or not. They avoid being committed to the project they took on while thinking they're contributing. Then there are people who aren't happy with the direction the project is taking, and perhaps never could be, so they either check out entirely or stick around to shoot everything down. Does this ring any bells? It does for me! Working together doesn't have to work this way.

When collaboration does work well, it is a gift.

While I've had some challenging learning experiences, I've had even more enchanting, life-changing experiences. I've forged many life-long friendships with women I've collaborated with in projects big and small. It's become my favorite way to get to know people, and community work has become a big part of how I socialize. I get to see how people act under pressure, live up to their commitments, how they give and take in relationships, and what kind of person they are.

I'm collaborating on a project that I'm very excited about. Nina Winter of TISSU Sewing Studio reached out to me to work with her on a fashion show featuring local creators that will celebrate diversity, creativity, and beauty in all shapes, colors, and sizes. This event will benefit Camp Destination Innovation, a career-development entrepreneurship summer camp for urban youth.

This collaboration has been magical. Working with Nina and getting to know her better has been a joy. She's so easy to work with and talk to. I must admit I'll be a bit disappointed when we don't have an excuse to meet. I stopped by to check in with her yesterday, and when I left, she gave me a surprise.

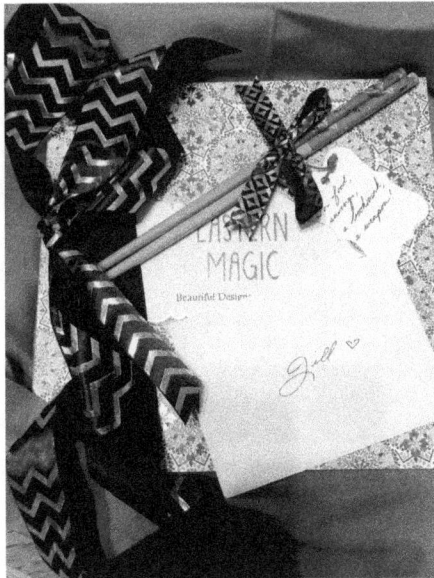

Sometimes the gifts are tangible

Sometimes the gifts of collaboration are tangible. Nina's sweet birthday gift of a book and fancy chopsticks with a note that they were to be used for "food, sewing, a bookmark, a weapon" delighted and moved me. Even when our project is done, I know I have gained a life-long friend from this experience.

The gifts of collaboration are plentiful when we approach it this way, coming together to create something bigger than we could ever do on our own. Rather than looking at group projects as something to be dreaded, we can see them as a way to build relationships to strengthen the community. That is the best gift of collaboration.

What will you do to be a better collaborator?

Worthy Women's Club

Unfortunately for me, I'm no good at saying "no." I have been working on turning my over-eager tendencies around with strategies I learned from the "Saying No" class we offer from time to time at the Finishing School for Modern Women. I am making progress. A big part of my problem is that I have a "fear of missing out," otherwise known as FOMO, which is such a common issue, scientists have studied it. Even when I was a child, I never wanted to go to bed, concerned that I'd miss out on something good. To this day, I still stay up too late.

So, when the Know Your Worth Women's Leadership conference chair asked me to be the conference co-chair, I really had to think about it. I'd already written the email in my head, declining the offer, when I ran into her at an awards banquet put on by the local Chamber of Commerce. The more I thought about it, the more I realized it was something too good to say "no" to. I was right. Collaborating with a team of 14 dedicated, influential, brilliant women was an enriching experience. So much so that I agreed to do it again.

Magic happens when we're together, and the Know Your Worth Conference has powerful juju. Connecting with other women to exchange ideas, solve problems, work on ourselves, and laugh is powerful. At the conference, I saw women open up and share their thoughts with complete strangers, to walk away feeling stronger and more connected as sisters.

We need our sisters

As we mature and get busier, it's harder to make and maintain female friendships. I think this happens for many reasons, and usually more than one.

- Women who had close female friends when they were younger lose touch with these friends when marriage, babies, and life become a more significant part of their lives.
- Women lose touch with women work friends when they change jobs and don't find the time to keep up with these friends when they aren't at work together anymore.
- Some women felt more comfortable with their male friends when they were younger and never forged close relationships with other women.
- Moving to other cities for work or marriage takes women away from the friends they grew up with. Finding the time and resources to make new friends besides ones at work gets more complicated when we're busy with our careers.
- As we get older and lose our close long-time friends, we aren't sure where to go to make new ones, as if a new

friend could ever give the same depth and history as the one we've lost.

I believe these are the reasons we isolate ourselves and give up on nurturing relationships that go beyond acquaintances. But while these rationalizations sound reasonable, what they ignore is how much we need each other. Taking the risk of being vulnerable and asking someone out on a "girlfriend date" is so worth the effort!

Because, as we get older, we need our sisters more than ever.

They are there for us in crisis and celebration – divorces, deaths, and loss; good times, successes, and minor miracles. Our women friends inspire, encourage, and support us to take significant risks and say "enough is enough" when we need it. These friends slap us back to reality when we need it and help us navigate this crazy time on earth we call life.

I couldn't have accomplished much of what I've been able to do or thrived through the crushing blows I've been dealt if it weren't for my sisters.

We all need a network of women in our professional lives too. Men have their "good old boys" clubs. Men forge relationships outside the boardroom, usually on golf courses, country clubs, sporting events, and private clubs, like fraternities. These gatherings are where business gets done, and decisions are made on who will be successful and who will not. Unfortunately, these are places where women usually aren't included, keeping us from serious business transactions and conversations.

As women, we need to come together and support each other too. But rather than our club being about excluding people, let's make our club about empowering each other and lifting each other up.

Instead of a Good Old Boys Club, we can have a Worthy Women's Club!

Now, this isn't an organization you can join. The Worthy Women's Club is an informal coming together of women who can help each other be more successful. Just like finding "mentors," we have to find the right fit, women we can collaborate with. We have to put ourselves out there, work together and see who we click with.

A big part of mastering how to say "no," is knowing when to say "yes." Agreeing to co-chair the Know Your Worth conference has helped me find new members for my own Worthy Women's Club. I'm excited to collaborate with them again for the conference next year and beyond.

Who is in your club?

Women Coming Together

It hasn't always been easy for me to be friends with women. When I was a girl, I remember feeling more comfortable with male friends than with female ones. I thought they were just easier to be around. But, looking back on this, I've realized the real reason I thought it was easier to be around the boys probably had more to do with how competitive and judgmental young women can be.

As young women, we learn to compete against each other for boys, attention, and recognition, and we're taught to estimate self-worth by comparing ourselves to others. But, as most adult women know, this competition can get ugly and downright mean. Even into my late 20s, I remember many times I felt I was treated worse by my women "friends" than I was by men. Although it was often because of men that we clashed.

In a way, it seems that we're pitted against each other. We are forced to compete, like gladiators, for the attention of lovers and more. Worst of all, we don't even realize this is happening. Every time we notice people comparing us to one another, we have a choice to look at these women as competition or acknowledge that we are in it together. Since these worthy women we're being compared to could be our support network, why not join up to fight our real oppressors together?

In my speech for our local Women's March in 2019, I made the statement, "The idea that women can't work together is bullshit!" I deliberated about using that line more than any other words in my speech, worried that the language was too strong. Finally, after a lot of thought, I decided, "Bullshit! That's exactly the punctuation this statement needs." Interestingly, it is the one that got the most applause and stuck with people the most. So much so that a group of local activists made a meme about it for social media.

I firmly believe that the way for us to step into our power is to stop competing and start practicing collaboration skills. Working together is the most effective way to make change happen in our personal and professional lives. Of course, I'm not saying this will be easy. Many people don't like group projects, for lots of reasons. But the excuses to avoid the occasional discomfort that comes from collaborating become meaningless when we look at the payoffs.

Women working together is powerful,
even virtually

By working with co-teachers at the Finishing School of Modern Women, I've been able to offer classes I couldn't have done on my own. I've also made new meaningful friendships with amazing women who have become valued members of my advisory council, the "Worthy Women's Club."

We have to learn to dance the Give and Take Tango to be good at collaborating. Successfully working together is as much about giving responsibility as it is taking responsibility. We must be willing to let go of control and delegate tasks, realizing that not only can other people accomplish the project as well as we can, but they may also be able to do it even better! We also can't wait for someone to ask us to take responsibility.

We must be willing to give our time and talents when it matters.

I don't think collaborating comes naturally to us humans. It takes diplomacy, the ability to recognize and value the needs of others, and stellar communication. If we're lucky, we learn these skills through studying, practicing, and learning from our mistakes. I am constantly amazed at the information we expect ourselves to know automatically. For example, we aren't born knowing how to drive a car, so why do we expect to understand how to be an effective communicator automatically?

Consciously working on how to have open interactions and tough conversations will pay off big time in your work with others.

As I've gotten older, I've learned to appreciate my women friends in a new way and love having more of them in my life. We don't compete. We support. As I look around and see all my strong women friends, I know why I am who I am today and what we can accomplish together.

How can you be a better friend to the women in your life?

Fierce Women

An event crossed my feed on Facebook that got my attention. Smaltz Brewing Company has brewed a special beer, She'Brew, to celebrate their birthday and the 100th anniversary of women's suffrage in New York. One hundred years! Part of the proceeds of this beer goes to Planned Parenthood and Pink Boots Society, a professional organization for women in the beer industry.

The brewery's pride in women's activism in New York makes me think about the history of my home state of Kansas in gaining rights for women. Did you know the first elected office ever held by a woman in the United States was in Argonia, Kansas? It's true! Her name is Susanna M. Salter, and she was elected mayor in 1887.

Her story is fascinating. She had no idea her name was entered into the race as a prank by a bunch of men. These men assumed Mrs. Salter would suffer a humiliating loss and thought this would teach women a lesson to keep them from running for office. Instead, she won with two-thirds of the vote.

One of the influences that inspired me to start the Finishing School for Modern Women is a book published by our independent bookstore, Watermark Books, called *"Radiating Like a Stone, Wichita Women, and the 1970s Feminist Movement."*

If you haven't read it, you should! This anthology of essays, compiled by the lifetime Wichita activist Myrne Roe, was written by 79 fierce local women who fought hard to make life better for all of us.

When I initially read the book, I noticed that some progress has been made, but was amazed at how many of these same issues still hold us back today. I decided then that the more we can own our power to follow our passions and dreams and persist despite the struggles, the more we create new opportunities for women.

My mom is fierce

My fierce role model is my mother pictured here as Rosie the Riveter at the 70th-anniversary historical fashion show we organized together for the National Federation of Press Women. Through her words and actions, my mother taught me that women are smart, powerful, and can achieve anything. When we come together, we achieve even more. She inspires me to be all I can be and help others do the same.

Who are your fierce female role models?

Are Friends Easier to Make as an Adult?

I've been thinking a lot about friendship lately. I listened to a story on NPR the other day about how hard it is to make friends as an adult and wondered how true this is for most people. I'm a naturally outgoing person who makes friends easily, and I didn't fully appreciate the struggle. So now I'm curious about this surprising superpower I didn't realize I had.

I've never lived anywhere other than my hometown, so maybe I don't truly understand what it would be like to *have* to make new friends. I'm still friends with people I met in elementary school! It would be hard to start over without having people close who know your history.

Our longtime friends remember the heroic and stupid things we've done, have the best dirt on us, and keep us humble by reminding us of where we came from. Besides, it's fun to relive some of the crazy stories of "Silly Things we did and Lived to Tell About."

Deep bonds happen from shared experiences between longtime friends that aren't the same as people you've just met. This closeness takes time, a precious commodity none of us have enough of.

Friends help us develop our worldview. The notion that our friends profoundly impact who we are has never struck me as hard as it did at the memorial of my brother's life. When Michael was a boy, he had a gang of close friends who hung around our house so much that they nearly felt like family. While they had grown apart and had falling outs at times, they all rallied when my brother sent up a flare to let them know his time was limited.

My geeky brother and his friend

Listening to the stories about what Michael meant in these marvelous men's lives gave me insight into my brother I hadn't seen. They described him as a goofy extrovert who brought together a bunch of extremely geeky, debilitatingly introverted boys and opened up a world to show them what was possible.

Michael's boyhood friends all gave him credit for the ways he influenced how they view life. As children, he convinced them to take risks and question the status quo. As adults, Michael introduced them to music, literature, and shows they would never have known about if it weren't for him. My brother always had thoughtful reasons around what he shared with people, passing along the philosophies and feelings that touched him, affecting how we view life ever after.

But life – and death change our friendships. We lose friends for all kinds of reasons, including outgrowing them at times. It's hard to know when to let go of friends that have become a habit rather than a joy. But remember, when something is draining all the joy out of your life, it's time to put the "Joy Suck Rule" into effect: "If something, or someone, is sucking the joy out of your life, it has to GO!"

Because, as we continue to grow and change, not everyone will board the same train as us. Some people take a different route or get stuck along the tracks, and that's okay. We can go back and visit these friends, but the different directions life has taken us makes it impossible to go back to the person we once were. Huzzah for that!

Part of reinvention is making new friends. A fun aspect of these new connections is you get to be around people who don't know all your past drama. Since they're just getting to know you, they don't have any expectations of who you are based on who you have been. With these new friends, you get to develop who you want to be.

Making new friends is also an opportunity to get to know people who are different than you, which is so much fun! Meeting people with different interests and ways of looking at the world is fascinating and helps us continue to grow.

I love having friends of different ages than me, absorbing the wisdom of my elders, and keeping current with my younger friends. Getting to know people from different races and cultures helps us see reality from varied perspectives and increases empathy. Making friends with people from different viewpoints, even political, helps us examine and solidify our own moral compass and accept that we all must live by our own principles and ethical standards.

Vivacious Marlene keeps me young

As usual, I took my curiosity to social media. I asked my friends if they think it's harder to make friends as adults. The results surprised me a bit. Out of the 95 comments on the post, 45% said it is harder to make friends now. That was higher than I thought it would be.

People found it more challenging to make friends because of time constraints, fewer situations to meet new people, and how much COVID cramped their style. We've missed seeing acquaintances out and about, and some friendships have slipped through the cracks during the past three years. Some said it has been a lifelong struggle to make true friends.

A smaller 34% said they'd disagreed that it's harder to make friends as an adult. Most of the respondents in this category were like me. Making new friends has always come easily to them. Some said that being more comfortable in their skin as an adult was a big reason they found it easier to connect.

That leaves the 21% that said it's different to make friends now compared to when they were children. They said they're more particular about who they let into their lives now and that a lack of free time to spend with their existing friends make them less likely to make new ones.

They also said it's harder to make genuine, quality friends as an adult since relationships take a long time to grow. The new relationships they make now are different than the ones they made earlier in life, and their requirements for intimacy within friendships have changed.

I may define friendships differently than most people. If I feel connected to you and like being around you, I consider you a friend. In a sociology class I took not long after high school, the professor described a true friend as someone who would answer your call and bail you out of jail in the middle of the night. He also said we're lucky if we have two or three of these kinds of friends during our entire lifetime.

Curiosity drove me to ask my friends on social media what they would do if I called at 3 AM and asked them to bail me out of jail. I have more than a few friends that, no matter the distance, would not only come get me if I called, but they'd also fight for me if needed.

I've been thinking about how I go about making friends and what recommendations I have for people who struggle with forming friendships. Here are my thoughts.

Meet new people with purpose.

One of my favorite ways to get to know people is through the volunteer and community actions I get involved in. Working with someone on a project is a great way to get to know them and to find out if you want to do anything with that person again! Coming together around a common cause helps us find like-minded people with at least one passion in common. It creates shared experiences, especially when the work is stressful. The relationships we make in these situations can last a lifetime.

Meet new people without leaving the house.

It's hard to make friends without leaving the house, though it isn't impossible. Many online forums and chat groups around specific interests bring people together in a way that works for even the most introverted. My geeky brother made connections that turned into friendships through these outlets. I've made many friends through social media that have turned into relationships offline.

Meet new people in a low-risk situation.

Part of why I started the Finishing School for Modern Women and love hosting the weekly Badass Women of Wichita Alliance events is because it brings women together. Every time we meet, I see people making new connections and friendships forming outside our events. We're meeting women who have just moved to Wichita or had other life changes and are looking for community. So if you're badass or want to be, you belong with us!

Friendships take time.

It's amazing when you meet someone you connect with that feels like magnets coming together, but that rarely happens. It takes shared experiences, facing adversity, and celebrating life to bring people closer. When you find someone you want to get to know, ask them to meet. It may feel a bit awkward, but if you mesh with that person, it can develop into the kind of long-term friends we treasure.

Not all relationships are the same.

Not every friendship has to turn into a love connection. Some people will never be "close" friends. That doesn't mean you don't have fun with them when you see them or that you can't find something to talk about.

In our Embracing Change workshop, we talk about the types of friends we need to be happy. We need Touch Stones that will bring us comfort and make us feel safe. Sounding Boards that you can consult about the things you're mulling over and get good advice. Frolickers that you can be spontaneous with that force you to have fun and don't let you take yourself too seriously. And the Truth Tellers that help you face the truth whether you ask them to or not. One person can rarely be all these things. Spread the love!

You're not going to be everyone's brand of disco.

If you don't end up clicking with everyone you meet, that's okay. Quality is more fulfilling than quantity in most situations. Rather than putting energy into why something didn't work, put the energy into trying again. It can be challenging to find people that can accept you for the freak that you are, but eventually, we find our people if we keep looking. Friends

186 ~ JILL D. MILLER

are people who make us feel like we belong, just as we are, and don't have to change to fit in.

Just relax and be yourself.

From working in sales for many years, I can tell you that the easiest way to build rapport and trust is to simply be yourself, quirks and all. People will either love and accept you for who you are or let you know they aren't worth your precious time and attention. If you can't let your freak flag fly with your friends, who can you show your uncensored realness to?

I value my relationships more than any possession I own and gladly accumulate friends before wealth. My friends have helped me through times when I couldn't make it on my own. They have forgiven me when I was thoughtless and supported and celebrated my successes. Maybe the significance I put on friendship is the real reason why it's easy for me to make friends. The treasures my friends bring to my life are worth the pain of the few with difficult endings. These experiences are all part of discovering how to choose friends worthy of our attention and learn to be better friends with those who are.

What will you do to add new friends to your life?

Chapter Seven

Never Finished Blooming

How We Thrive

1. Survival Skills

2. Silver Linings

3. Reinvention Is Badass

4. By the Numbers

5. Mind the Gap

6. Not for the Fainthearted

7. Manifest It!

Survival Skills

Always on the sunny side

It may be some kind of affliction I've never heard of, but when things get really tough, I tend to get optimistic. I don't start there. I began in denial in this recent life upside-down cake of the pandemic lockdown. "It can't happen here." (Remember that, Zappa fans?) Then went to anger. "How the hell did this happen?" Finally, I'm starting to hit resignation, "This is going to hurt, but it is not within my control." I've had a few meltdowns and some pity parties too. But, I can feel the optimism starting to build. And yes, I realize how obnoxious that makes me.

I get scared when under pressure, and I don't like being scared. At all. I will do nearly anything to avoid it, including calling it other names, like "worried" and "stressed." But it all boils down to the same emotion – fear.

When I worked for Aveda, my boss had a saying, "Motivated by fear." That resonated with me. After a brief stint in the fetal position, the fear kicks into high gear, inspiring me to figure out what can be done to tame the fear.

For some people, creating artwork or playing music brings them peace. I take comfort in problem-solving, finding workarounds, and creative solutions. Maybe it makes me feel like I have control over change, which I know isn't true. Focusing on solutions does change my attitude, though, and that helps.

No matter what the situation, coming up with feasible strategies helps me feel better about change. Having a plan gives me hope and optimism that things just might work out. That's when I start getting all obnoxiously positive about the future and want to share that hope.

Optimism is one of my happiest survival skills. This determination to keep going despite what the world throws at me has served me well. I have always had a little light of hope that lives inside me that refuses to be snuffed out. I'm grateful for this resilience and like to think it comes from my ancestors and their strength to face adversity.

I'm fascinated by the creative process and learning how to stretch our imaginations. Delving into what holds us back from being our most innovative selves, I discovered the "Myths of Creativity" by David Burkus. His Constraints Myth, the idea that having limited options makes it more challenging to create something meaningful, is especially on my mind lately. From this book, I learned that being confined in choices makes us more creative, giving us a direction to pursue rather than unlimited possibilities.

Figuring out how to work through this pandemic lockdown, which feels like being grounded as a child, will be incredibly challenging and a good exercise for our problem-solving prowess. We're all going through a roller coaster of emotions right now. No one can stay optimistic all the time, not even me.

Sometimes survival means taking things one day at a time, with an eye toward actions that will help in the future. Since we don't know what will happen next, this is the approach we'll have to take for now. Things are changing so fast that we just have to wait things out a bit to see what happens. Combining optimism with creativity will help us persevere. Here are some survival ideas to try when chaos knocks.

Don't pay attention to all the rumors.

Whenever there's a crisis, lots of crazy rumors go around, online and person-to-person. When the pandemic started, I got messages from social media friends with dire warnings that sounded like conspiracy theories and no way to tell where the news originated. The messages were scary and may not be completely accurate.

We have to be careful about passing along reactionary information. Some factions want to keep us scared, and spreading misinformation is one of the ways they make that happen. Check the sources of the information to make sure they're reputable and that there's more than one source carrying the story.

It's okay to disconnect.

It's important to stay informed, but it's also important to disconnect sometimes. Take a break from social media and the news. Read a synopsis of what was televised rather than watching the whole thing. Believe me, if something important happens, you'll hear about it.

Be gentle with yourself.

In times of uncertainty, emotions run high, especially if you're empathic and absorb the feelings of people around you. At the Finishing School for Modern Women, we recognize that there aren't bad and good emotions; they're all just emotions. All these feelings have information to give us and lessons to teach us. We avoid the feelings we don't want to think about by keeping ourselves extra busy, so we don't have time to sit with our emotions and let ourselves feel and think about them.

Sound overwhelming? When there are so many emotions to contend with at one time, it's hard to know where to start. I'll never forget the wisdom my neighbor, Cindy Watson, Senior Pastor of the First Methodist Church, gave me right after my friend Tanya Tandoc was murdered. When she asked how I was feeling, I told her I was going back and forth between sadness and anger and didn't know what to do with that. She told me, "Focus on the sadness. The anger will take care of itself." It was good advice.

Dealing with all these feels is ridiculously hard, especially when life is extra stressful. So it's essential to look for resources to help in tough times. One of my go-to places is *"Mindful Magazine."* They've put together resources covering everything from feeling isolated to stopping worry. I plan to spend some time there myself.

Try to have some fun.

It's easy to get stuck in the gloom and doom. If we could change situations simply by worrying, spending our energy ruminating about what may happen would make sense. I know this is easier said than done to let these stressors go. There is a lot to worry about right now.

I'm going to try to do something fun every day as part of my self-care during COVID. For example, last night, I joined some friends for a virtual cocktail party. We all logged onto an online meeting with a drink in hand and just talked. As an extroverted introvert, this "social" distancing will not be easy, and I'll need to get creative to stay sane.

We'll get through this.

Weathering an epidemic will be tough, but we are going to survive. The more we can come together to help each other, the better.

There has never been a more critical time to support local businesses. While we can't dine at restaurants, we can get take-out. We can't shop at local shops, but we can buy from them online, their social media profiles, and contact them for private video shopping sessions. There are lots of birthdays in April, and we'll need presents. Those of us born under the outgoing sign of Aries are being punished enough by having to self-isolate.

What have you found works best for you when in survival mode, and how can you use these tactics again when times get tough?

Silver Linings

Well, I warned you! I've told you that I tend to look for the positives when things get tough. It makes me feel better to know that there is some light in all the gloom and doom we're feeling now. While I realize it's pretty obnoxious, I can't help myself. It gives me hope.

I'm not the only one looking for silver linings through the isolation of quarantine. Have you seen the videos about how the planet is healing itself while we're all staying home? It's amazing. I'm seeing beautiful stories about kind acts and how people are getting creative to show their love. The crazy family-made videos are my favorites. It's interesting to see what people will come up with to stay entertained.

Three big cheers for the internet! Can you imagine life without it? Being online keeps me from being cut off from humanity, which is tough on your social butterfly friend. I asked my friends on social media recently, "Have you discovered any silver linings yet? What are they?" I mainly got "yes" responses. Here's what they had to say.

Slowing Down

Many people said they're grateful that their lives have slowed down a bit, giving them time to reflect on what and who is important. People have time to read, go for walks, have real sit-down meals, and dig in the dirt. Suddenly there's time to work on projects, like writing a book or learning a new skill.

Creatives are coping by making art in whatever way pleases them. It's been beautiful to see how, when times get tough, people turn to the arts for comfort. We need to remember this consolation and appreciate the people who do the work usually taken for granted.

Nesting

All my stress cleaners and overachievers are going to work on their homes. People are getting projects done they've been putting off for years. (Not me.) Too bad there's no place to take items to donate because people are organizing their houses and purging like crazy. (I have done a bit of that, but mainly because I needed to find something.)

My coworker got bored during an
online meeting

Connecting

I've had lots more phone conversations with family and friends I haven't seen in a while. My friends have done the same. When things go off-kilter, I want to pull my people closer. So I've been checking in on people I know who are alone or might need help.

Families, especially teenagers, are grateful for their time to-gether. Couples are spending more time with each other, moti-vating predictions of the next baby boom. And the pets are either confused or ecstatic. Sadly, they're going to have a hard time when we start leaving home again.

Adapting

I recently found a HUGE silver lining, and I'm damn excited about it. I realized something I would never have known if I hadn't had to adapt to the coronavirus. We had our first live online Finishing School for Modern Women class! I was blown away at how great it worked. It was especially fun to have my mom and sister in attendance. They were hilarious, and I loved seeing their faces. I'm excited that our far-flung friends can also come to play with us!

I would never have realized this if I hadn't had to adapt to a business climate that's changing faster than the speed of light. I didn't want to shut down when we needed to come together the most and have a little extra time to invest in ourselves. While this is likely a stopgap until we can meet in person again, it is a fun possibility to explore.

What silver linings have you found, and how have you adapted this to your life presently?

Reinvention Is Badass

One of the reasons I've loved being a business development consultant for over 20 years is that my work is ever-changing. I never know what new challenges await when people come to me to help them start or grow their businesses. Since I don't specialize in one kind of business, I've helped clients with companies in industries I'd never have imagined, from aerospace registration auditors to death doulas.

It's an exciting stretch to learn about new industries and companies. I don't get the chance to get bored because working with such a variety of focuses expands my view of the world of business. I've seen consultants with specific specialties get stuck offering the same solutions to every client as they did when they started consulting. Pretty soon, they can't "see the forest for the trees," as the old proverb goes.

By staying open to lots of new information and focusing on the bigger picture view – the forest, we can see beyond the trees to form new connections and see solutions other people miss. This is the creative side of business that I love the most. Finding ways to do things that haven't been tried before is risky. It takes courage – but so does being an entrepreneur.

I've discovered that reinvention is vital to longevity in my business and personal life. The companies that desperately hang onto how they've continuously operated no matter what happens eventually fall behind. People who aren't willing to have some flexibility to change their minds forfeit the present moment's happiness. Living in the past keeps us from seeing the possibilities of right now.

In the entrepreneurship classes I took in college, I learned about the business lifecycle. Businesses only grow for so long and then hit the "maturity" stage. Then, just like in life, the business cycle is all downhill from there. From maturity, the next part of the cycle is decline. Unless action is taken and innovation or change occurs, the next stage is death – or waiting to die, as many companies do. I think humans get caught in that loop too.

Taking small risks by trying what I call "experiments" is a way to ease into change. Put a toe in the water and see how it feels. If you don't like it, you can back up. But if it feels good, it's time to move a little deeper. Before you know it, you're swimming with sharks in the deep end! Trying new strategies eases transitions and gives insights into navigating the waters and avoiding undertows. It also breathes new life into stagnant situations.

The possibilities are endless

COVID has shaken our snow globe hard. It's taken so much of what we've taken for granted and turned it upside down. It shows us proof-positive that the idea that we can control what happens is an illusion. There are people stubbornly fighting to return to the status quo. I get it. Change is scary, and it's hard. But, refusing to change when the world is changing all around us is a sure route from maturity to death. Like it or not – change is inevitable.

I've been struggling hard with what to do with the Finishing School for Modern Women through the pandemic. It became apparent that offering live classes during a plague was not a sustainable business strategy. I've tried some experiments over the past year, some results I've liked better than others. But, I'll continue to try different ideas because I'm stubbornly not ready to give up on my mission to help women own their power.

The biggest hurdle has been to decide what I want the Finishing School to become. What has always been important to me is bringing women together to collaborate and make us all stronger. I still can't believe in 2021 how hard we still have to fight for our fundamental rights as humans and citizens of the world. We've got to come together, especially now, to fight for an equal playing field for all people.

I must remember to be extremely careful in what I ask for because it's startling how often what I request comes to pass. Earlier this year, I thought about what organizations I could work with to reinvent the Finishing School. I put a toe in and approached a few people, but it wasn't the right fit.

Then, out of the blue, a local brewpub, the PourHouse by Walnut River Brewing Company, contacted me. The general manager had an idea to start a women's empowerment initiative on Monday evenings and thought I might be able to help. The result: the Badass Women of Wichita Alliance!

BADASS WOMEN
of Wichita
ALLIANCE

What is a Badass Woman? Glad you asked. A badass woman is a resilient, confident, bold woman who knows her mind. She is sexy, funny, does what she wants, and doesn't need anyone's approval. Being a badass is about knowing your own worth and not letting anyone else mess with that. It's about taking control and becoming the best version of yourself.

So, we have the use of the Pourhouse's spacious private meeting space and delicious free food every Monday evening. We invite women of all ages to join our inclusive society for discussions and actions that build community, empower women, and develop our badassery.

On the first Monday of each month, we work on our badassery skills with a Finishing School for Modern Women workshop focused on various empowering topics we'll announce in advance. We have panel discussions, table topic discussions, and mini-workshops to keep things fun and interactive.

Once a month, we have a Fun-Raiser for a local nonprofit that supports women and families. These events won't be a typical fundraiser rubber chicken dinner. We're way too badass for that! We suggest a $10 donation with additional donations accepted at the door.

We've had "Moms of Media Trivia Night" to raise money for MamaFilm, an arts organization that elevates the voice of storytellers through a maternal gaze. We've played The "Price is Right" game for a fun-raiser for the Kansas Food Bank. To raise money for a summer camp for LGBTQ+ children, we had a "S'More Friends" party and made friendship bracelets, posters to welcome the campers, and of course, s'mores.

Other weeks of the month, we invite community organizations, professional associations, and nonprofits that support women and families to get involved and work together to broaden our community of women helping women.

The Society of Women Engineers practiced their presentation for their national conference, and Soroptimist International told us about all the scholarships and programs they have to support women. We're always looking for these groups so we can help shine a light on what they're doing to help build their organization.

We get creative to fill any gaps in the schedule. For example, we've had speed mixers for women business owners to spread the word about what they're doing and badass dance parties so we can blow off a little steam. Coming up with unique ideas every week is challenging – and fun.

While these events are developed around issues and topics specific to women, all genders are welcome. We love men and value their alliance and respect.

When I started thinking about reinventing the Finishing School, I realized it would take time for the right situation to come along. In my wildest imagination, it didn't occur to me that working with a brewpub would be the solution I was seeking. It goes to show that being open to unexpected solutions and being flexible is key to reinvention.

Another thing I learned about the business life cycle in entrepreneurship classes is that rebirth is the only way to save your business from the downward spiral from maturity to certain death. The way to revive your business and bring it back to the growth stage is to come up with a strategy innovative enough to give new life to your business. Already I'm noting that there's a lot of excitement around being a badass woman, which is exciting and energizing. My reinvention is truly badass.

What does being a badass mean to you? Do you think of yourself as a badass?

By the Numbers

I know many powerful women who are accomplished and brilliant in so many ways – except when it comes to money. They don't want to deal with their finances, so they don't. Some are married, so they turn all the responsibility over to their partner. Others hire accountants to take care of their financial business, so they don't have to think about it. Others ignore their finances until they can't be ignored any longer. Some people are so stymied by bill-paying that they don't open their mail and then watch mountains of paper pile up.

The problem with ignoring your situation is that it will get you into trouble. Not paying attention to what is going on with your finances can make you vulnerable in many ways. It may seem safe to turn your business over to someone you trust, but circumstances change. People leave our lives, make mistakes or bad decisions, or may have trouble talking about tough subjects, like cash flow problems. Some people get greedy, are dishonest, and don't think about how using your cash will hurt you.

Mountains of mail become bill avalanches that only get worse with penalties and interest. It gets expensive when we aren't paying attention.

When times are hard, we don't want to deal with money worries, afraid of what we'll find. Sometimes the circumstances aren't as dire as we think, especially when we stay on top of it. Sometimes it's worse, but at least when you know what's going on, you can make a plan. When times are good, we don't think we need to pay as close attention to our expenses. That's when spending goes wild!

Managing finances gets even more complicated when you're a business owner. Now you have two sets of accounts to balance and bills to pay! You have to pay attention to finances when you're the Boss Lady. After all, the measurement of business is money.

Knowing how to read financial reports, like Profit and Loss statements, are vital to understanding financial health and business trends. That is if the business owner actually does the work to make the reports happen and cracks the code to know what the numbers mean. One of the most important, but somehow most intimidating, skills you need to succeed in business is wealth management.

One of the best ways to own our power and be more successful in life is to be a better money manager. In fact, not being a good money manager often makes people victims. There are too many stories of celebrities and lottery winners, people with what must have seemed like a bottomless pot of gold, losing it all by not paying attention. I'm not saying you have to do all the work, but it is imperative to check in regularly to be aware and informed about your situation.

Lots of people have an aversion to numbers. I've been there myself. I've always been more of a creative than an analytical thinker. But just like I've practiced being a better writer and teacher, I've found that, with practice, I can be good with finance too. First, I needed to get out of my own way. For some people, it's a lack of knowledge. For others, it's fear of numbers, emotions tied to money, or never having enough money to manage. I think I've had them all!

To get out of our way, we must consider our attitudes and beliefs toward wealth. Money isn't just money. Money represents power, love, joy, and much more. For some, wealth means power or respect, and they think that money gives control. For others, it's happiness or freedom, the idea that having enough resources will solve all of life's problems. While some people equate money with love and security, feeling that cash will make people love them more or keep them safer.

What does money mean to you? What emotions do thoughts of money bring up for you; feelings of worry, guilt, anger, sadness, power, love, or joy? Since the attitudes about money were shaped in childhood by our parents, what did money represent in your family when you were growing up, and what were you taught about its uses? Did your parents fight about money? Use the money to control you or one another? Use the money to show love?

By considering what money means to us, we can see what values we have attached to wealth. Values are the standards that we use to measure ourselves and underlie everything we are and do. If what we value isn't aligned with how we define success in our lives, then everything based on those values will be out of whack.

Everything we think and feel about a situation stems from how valuable we perceive it to be. When the way someone measures their worth in the world is solely financial, that is what will drive all their decisions and worldview. On the other hand, I've known people who thought money is evil and have done everything to avoid it. Neither approach works or is a healthy way to look at finance.

When we know our values, we can ask ourselves important questions: Why do I feel such a need for this value in the first place? How am I choosing to measure success/failure for myself? These questions can be uncomfortable to answer but will help you find out how to get out of your own way. You can begin by reframing how you look at success and measure it.

I think it's as important for everyone to be as literate with numbers as with words, so we offer a series of classes at the Finishing School for Modern Women based on the FDIC National Standards for Adult Financial Literacy Education. These standards identify the personal finance knowledge and skills an adult should have: "Mistress of Money," "Queen of Credit" and the "Empress of Investments." The FDIC.gov website is a treasure trove of resources to help you with these skills.

For business owners and directors of nonprofit organizations, we offer "Boss Lady" to help them discover how to read financial statements and make these reports their friends, along with other strategies to build a superhero business!

But the best financial advice I can offer you is, don't bury your head in the sand when it comes to money. Figure out what it is that's holding you back, learn the skills you need to be a better money manager, and face it head-on. I guarantee keeping track of where you are financially will bring you more success and peace of mind. Try it and see.

What does money mean to you?

Mind the Gap

This week I took a little road trip to Lindsborg, Kansas, to speak at the Kansas Women Attorney Association conference. Wichita attorney Gaye Tibbets and I led a breakout session on the gender wage gap and how we can work to close it.

According to the Institute for Women's Policy Research, in 2017, women still make only 80 cents for every dollar earned by men, a gender wage gap of 20 percent. This gap is even wider for women of color. Hispanic women have the lowest wage equity, making 43 percent less than white men and 28 percent less than white women.

Where you live also has a bearing on how women are paid. My hometown, Wichita, has bigger wage equity issues than the national average. A Wichita Eagle article in March 2018 reported that Wichita ranks in the bottom 20 percent of similarly sized cities for wage equality, coming in at just 72 cents to every dollar.

It takes community working together
to make changes

Gaye presented some eye-opening statistics. Although the Equal Pay Act of 1963 makes it illegal to pay different wages for equal work, requiring equal skill, effort, and responsibility, performed under similar working conditions, Gaye showed us how the disparity still exists.

Even in cases where the demographics, such as marital status, number of children, and universities attended are the same, one year out of college, women still earn only 82 percent, compared to men in similar jobs. The most discouraging statistic to me is how this is getting worse, not better. According to trendlines set in 2001, it will be 2152 before there is equal pay if things continue the same way as they are now.

So, what can we do? One thing we can do is learn to be better negotiators! Did you know that 20 percent of adult women (22 million people) say they never negotiate at all, even when they know they should? When women do negotiate for salaries, they're less optimistic about how much is available, so they typically ask for and get less – 30 percent less than men. Now, don't get me wrong. I'm not saying this gender pay gap is all on us and our ability to negotiate, but this is one of the most powerful things we can learn and practice.

Part of the reason I started the Finishing School for Modern Women is to help women step into their power. Financial power is a big part of that. Our class on negotiating, Getting What You Want, is one of my favorites because of all the success stories I get from women who take it. We don't have to negotiate the same way as men, even when negotiating with men. We have different strengths that we can use to our advantage. For example, our superpower of insight into others' feelings is a crucial negotiating skill.

Like everything else, preparation is 90 percent of what makes negotiations successful. We must know what we want before we can negotiate for it. An excellent place to start is researching your state's Department of Labor's wage survey, which gives pay rates for experienced and entry-level positions throughout the state.

Doing this research will help determine where to start negotiations and what the walk-away point will be. Sure, it will be five or ten minutes of discomfort to bring up the conversation, but it could pay off in hundreds of thousands of dollars over your career.

Being a successful negotiator takes practice. What will you do to get more practice asking for what you want?

Not for the Fainthearted

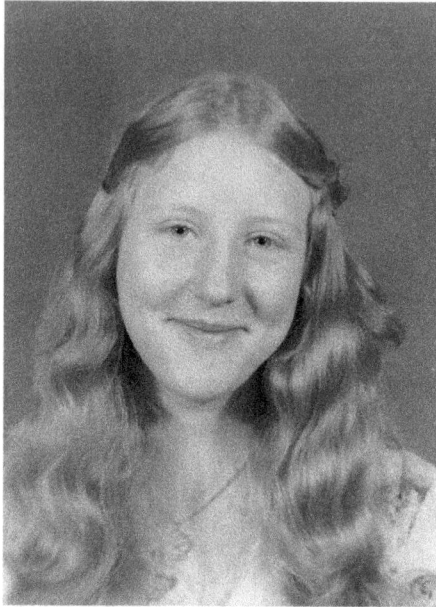

In my head, I will always be this teenager, although the mirror tells me a different story. Not that I mind getting older. I don't. As I get older, the more comfortable and confident I feel in my skin. Through this transition, I'm learning to let go of other people's opinions of me, good and bad, and listen to my inner wisdom.

Still, getting older is not for the fainthearted. Changes to our bodies are a normal part of aging. Maybe it helps us realize that we're mortal and time is fleeting, so we'd better take full advantage of what time we have. Unfortunately, it seems we trade physical pain for the emotional pain we had when we were younger. I don't like the aches and pains that go along with aging. I realize now that everywhere we hurt ourselves when we're younger will turn into arthritis later. If I'd known that, I probably wouldn't have been so demanding with my body and treated myself better.

This isn't the only way I wish I'd had treated myself better. I had an interesting conversation over lunch this week with two women I admire and respect. We talked about what we wish we could go back and tell our younger selves. Here's what we would say:

- Lighten up! You don't have to be so serious all the time, or hard on yourself.
- Enjoy the moments! Memories you make along your life are what make life worth living.
- Trust yourself! You had it right the first time, so stop second-guessing yourself and listen to your intuition.
- Take care of yourself first and foremost! You are responsible for your own happiness, so when you don't like something in your life, know that you can change it.
- Some relationships are not sustainable! People will come and go from your life, and that's okay.
- Not everyone has the capacity to have a healthy, loving relationship! No matter how much you wish it were different. It doesn't make that person bad, just not for you.
- You don't have to be nice to people who are trying to hurt you! Sometimes walking, or running, away is the best thing to do.

To feel more comfortable in our skin, healing from the past takes strength and isn't for the fainthearted. Part of how we make that happen is by learning to go back and nurture the child within.

What would you say to a younger you?

Manifest It!

I first learned about manifesting when I was in my 30s. I had friends who believed they could think their way into what they wanted, so I couldn't resist teasing them a little. I told a fib to a friend that I had started visualizing where I would park in crowded lots to find a better space. When my friend told me that she tried it and it really helped her get a closer parking space, I decided to actually try it. Since then, I've become a believer in the law of attraction. But in all my years since, I've never seen someone attract anything as powerfully as my mom did when she manifested a new dog recently.

Not long ago, my mom's ancient, disoriented dog got out of the house and never came back. We spent days scouring the neighborhood, but that dog was long gone. My mom is usually pretty stoic, but she took that loss super hard and has felt mopey since. Coming to my office to work with my staff has helped distract her a bit, but she's been biding her time for a new pup until the weather gets better in the spring.

When the days started getting warmer, Mom decided it was time to start thinking about getting a dog again. She stalked the Humane Society and rescue group websites but was discouraged about her chances of getting a dog through an organization since she doesn't have a fenced-in yard. Her rescue odds were even slimmer because her husband requested they get a poodle since they don't shed and definitely not a puppy.

Even though she didn't feel like getting out of the house, Mom dragged herself to a workshop I taught on embracing change for the Badass Women of Wichita Alliance earlier this month. For one of the class exercises, everyone was to write a power statement about a change they had the power to control. On cards I handed out, I asked everyone to fill in the blanks that said, "I want to_____, so I can_____. My first step is_____."

I wasn't surprised when my mom said, "I want a dog so that I can be happy again." Mom has been part of many conversations about manifesting from hanging out in my office, but what she had written as her first step surprised me. She said, "Since I probably can't get a dog through a rescue group, I'll have to wait until a dog falls into my lap. So I'm putting it into the Universe and see what happens."

Immediately, the woman across the table from her said, "I have a dog that I need to rehome. He's an eight-year-old poodle mix named Larry." She pulled out her phone to show us pictures, or we may not have believed it was true. We were shocked and could hardly believe she got so lucky so effortlessly. All she did was put it out there, and everything she asked for came to be.

Several days later, we picked up Larry and brought him to his new home. He's the perfect dog! Larry is smart, sweet, and already trained. Mom lucked out just by asking for what she wanted in the right place and time. It was amazing. It wouldn't have happened if she hadn't come to the workshop.

Was this a magical, mystical occurrence that got my mom her dog? I don't think so. The skeptic that tempted me to tease my friends about what I thought was an oobie doobie idea of "manifesting" is still with me. I have a theory about the law of attraction and how you can make your dreams a reality.

Larry, the dog my mom manifested, is awesome

Define what you want.

How can you get what your heart desires when you aren't clear about what that means? The first step is to clearly define what it is you want. I believe this is the most important step, and the easiest to screw up. So take some time to think and dig deep because this tactic alone will take you far.

Be careful what you ask for!

We have a running joke in our office, "Be careful what you wish for! It may come true!" For example, when I had ankle surgery, I thanked friends who helped me by posting pictures of the meals they brought over while I was balancing on one leg. So many people told me, "I wish I could have surgery so everyone would bring me food!" Nope! I assured people that there are better ways to get some TLC and home cooking than recovering from surgery. Don't even put those kinds of thoughts out there!

Be specific.

The more complete a picture you have in mind, the closer you'll get to what you actually crave, not a cheap imitation. Frame what you're looking for with the same concepts as setting SMART goals. Make your vision specific, measurable, attainable with a stretch, relevant to you, and time-bound when appropriate.

Plant it!

Plant the specifics of what you would like to manifest securely in your brain. Write it down, think about it, and visualize what you yearn for. The object of the game is to get these thoughts anchored into your subconscious so your brain can work on your goals when you're not even thinking about them.

Make a self-fulfilling prophecy.

I believe a big part of manifesting what you need is self-fulfilling prophesy, the idea that describing a prediction can cause it to come true. I believe that whether we realize it or not when we focus on what we want, our minds start noticing more patterns and possibilities. Our brains subconsciously help move us closer toward making our dreams come true. It's much like never noticing a specific car model until you think you might buy one, then what was once invisible becomes the only car you see.

Put it out into the world.

Once you're clear on what you want, start talking to people about it. You never know what will happen. My mom would still be waiting for a dog to come into her life if she hadn't talked about it.

The first people I talk to about my vision are the ones I think will be allies in helping me achieve my goals. I want to plant ideas in their subconscious too. It may be a bit of serendipity, but once I hear about something, it's amazing how often that same topic will come up again from unrelated sources.

Let it go.

Remember the scene in Mary Poppins when the children created a job description of precisely what they were looking for in a nanny? Then, when the list was torn up and tossed into the fireplace, the smoke carried the children's desires on the wind to Mary Poppins, who, of course, was "practically perfect in every way" for the job.

Whatever your beliefs are – praying about what you need, turning it over to the Divine, becoming receptive to the assistance of the Sage, or sending it out into the Universe – I believe this is another important aspect of manifesting. While I said earlier that I don't believe manifesting is a mystical process, I believe that having the faith to put trust in a Higher Power is the best way to let go of control. Trying to force things to work out the way we think they should rarely ends well and keeps us from seeing better opportunities.

You have the power to change anything you don't love about your life. Manifest what makes you happy!

What is your power statement?

Chapter Eight

Never Finish Fighting

How We Become Fierce Women

1. When Women Lead

2. Quitting Time

3. Celebrating Women

4. Taking a Stand

5. What Are Your Superpowers?

When Women Lead

I clearly do not know how to say "no." In my short bio of 50 words or less, I include the description "zealous volunteer" since this is a big part of who I am. Even though we have a class about saying "no" at the Finishing School for Modern Women, I've found that all too often, the best answer is "yes." I said "yes" to being the Chair of the Friends of the Wichita Art Museum (FWAM for short) and on the Board of Trustees because I've been a big fan of the museum since I was a youngster and want to lend my hand and brainpower to an institution I love. Of course, it didn't hurt that I would have the chance to work with a leader that I respect, admire, and know I could learn from.

I also had to say "yes," when asked to co-chair the Know Your Worth Women's Leadership Conference. The mission is to help women know their worth and own their power, which is precisely aligned with my mission and beliefs. The incredible women I'd be working with sealed the deal.

In the "Saying No" class, we talk about when it's important to say "yes." The class handout includes a checklist of questions to ask yourself when deciding to take on another project. A couple of the items on the list that are the most important to me are "What do I most want to learn from this experience?" and "What will I gain from doing this?"

We often think volunteering needs to be something entirely altruistic, spending our scarce spare time giving to others without any expectations of how it might benefit us. I've started to look at this differently. I'm busier than I need to be, and my time is precious, so to spend time on projects, they have to take me closer to my goals or have some other kind of benefit.

So, when I heard the United WE in Kansas City was planning to bring its Appointments Project training to Wichita, I was interested in listening to their thoughts on saying "yes." This training is especially timely since I had a decision to make. I had just been asked to serve on the Innovation Committee for the strategic plan for Wichita State University and wasn't sure if I wanted to take on one more thing.

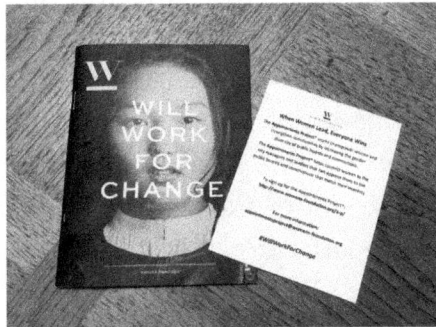

United WE helps women get appointed
to positions to create change

I learned more about the United WE and met the president and CEO of this organization earlier this year when she was the keynote speaker for the 2018 Know Your Worth conference. Started in Kansas City in 1991, this nonprofit is dedicated to promoting equity and opportunity for the economic well-being of women and their families.

The United WE has done extensive research in Kansas, Missouri, and Oklahoma to understand better the issues women face today, so they can pinpoint barriers to success and figure out how to make lasting and measurable changes. (Go to their website at united-we.org to read their research. Warning: It's dismal news.)

United WE does tons of great work on issues important to women of all ages, like wage equity and helping change public policies affecting women. One of the ways they're working to create change is by helping women become better represented in the places that make policy.

The Appointments Project does this by helping women get appointed to civic boards and commissions that match their strengths and interests. Having more women in these positions gives us a stronger voice to start conversations about the barriers and work toward creating solutions and equality.

If you live in one of the states United WE serves, simply go to the Appointments Project website, fill out a form and submit your resume. They can help you research which boards and committees fit you best. Once approved, you'll be part of the organization's talent database, which they reference when told of opportunities. Since the United WE doesn't charge anything to help, why not take advantage of their expertise, experience, and connections?

Of course, you don't have to go through the United WE to get on a civic board or commission. You can apply yourself by researching which boards have openings. Search the internet for your city, county, or state and "civic board and commission openings" to find a list of all the openings, usually arranged by category, so you can easily find what interests you. Some appointments have to come from recommendations from a local elected official. Don't let that stop you! Reach out and ask for a meeting to introduce yourself as a worthy candidate.

Have you thought about giving your time, experience, and expertise but don't know where to start? Maybe serving on a government board doesn't do it for you? While the Appointments Project is predominately for work on boards and commissions, there are many other ways to get involved in the community. Believe me, there are no nonprofit organizations anywhere in the world that aren't looking for people to help!

You don't even have to commit to being on a board to do it. Volunteering for limited or one-time events can be a blast.

Great way to get out of the house, meet new people, and get the warm fuzzy feelings you get from volunteering. Search for volunteer opportunities near you to find portals like Volunteer Kansas that list volunteer opportunities based on your interests.

Not only are you doing something good for others when you volunteer, but you're also getting the chance to refine skills you may not get the opportunity to do through your job. Serving in a leadership position in a volunteer organization is a way for you to try on or refine new skills to learn to be a better boss lady.

The best part of being the chair of a board is that you have an entire executive board, along with past chairs, to help mentor, give advice, and make decisions, so you're not all alone at the top like it can feel when you get promoted at a J. O. B. The good decisions I've made as chair of the Friends of the Wichita Art Museum have been because of the advice of everyone on the board, and I am grateful for their support.

If you're thinking, "I couldn't possibly do anything like that!" I ask you, why not? You have everything you need right now to be fabulous. You can learn what the organization does and form intelligent opinions and action plans. Learning to speak our truth is a big part of owning our power, and your truth is just as important as anyone else's. So, take a risk. Get out there. Do something!

By the way, of course, I said "yes" to the Innovation Committee.

How can you become more involved in your community?

Quitting Time

I got to do one of my favorite things last week. I moderated a panel discussion for the Women SCORE Higher Conference sponsored by the Service Corp of Retired Executives, aka SCORE. The conference's theme was Healthy Mind, Body & Business, and the panel discussion was all about "Coming into Balance." The conversation was a lot of fun and chock full of insights about burnout and tips for how to stop being a victim to the grind of everyday life.

I love participating in panel discussions because you never know what new perceptions will pop up. Listening to the opinions of several people answering the same question is insightful, whether the answers build on each other or are entirely different. One of my biggest takeaways from the session was saying "no" and letting go — two things I am notoriously bad at doing.

One of the panelists suggested having a list of criteria, or a rubric, that she uses to help her make decisions about what she'll say "yes" to, which is an excellent, structured way of avoiding getting in over your head. But, the biggest gem I discovered was from an audience question — "What do I do if I've said yes to things I shouldn't have, and now I'm drowning?" Everyone on the panel agreed; sometimes, you simply have to let go and move on.

Right now is an excellent time to decide what to give up. COVID has changed so much over the past two years. So, this pause is a fantastic opportunity to look at what was working and not working before and make changes — that includes rethinking all the projects we've hung onto for years. I recently had drinks with a friend I worked with on the huge ArtAID fundraiser for 20 years. While it was an awe-inspiring event with an extravagant fashion show and art auction that raised over $1.5 million, we were shocked at how long that event kept going, especially after we should have moved on.

These conversations have me thinking – if we can have a rubric for when to say "no," we can also create criteria to know when to let go. I need this because I've always had a hard time knowing when to quit. I got it in my head a long time ago that quitting is a bad thing, so I'll try to keep things going even when it's past time to stop.

I obviously need an objective tool to help me. After choosing my criteria for the rubric I rate each item on a scale of one to five, with five being the highest end of the scale. When I'm finished, I add up the numbers to see where the numbers fall. Here are the criteria I've come up with.

When was the last time this project brought me joy?

Someone close to me reminded me recently of my "Joy Suck" rule – when anything is sucking the joy out of my life, it has to go! It's a good rule to keep in mind, and I couldn't believe I needed that reminder.

Am I continuing this project out of a sense of duty, or am I stuck?

Continuing to work on something because you think you should will turn any project into an uninspired drudge that usually doesn't work for anyone involved. Feeling numb can be a strong signal you're not fully engaged. So let go and open up the position for someone else who will be inspired by a new challenge and move on to something new to reignite your spark. Term limits on boards exist for a good reason.

Do the reasons to step away outweigh the reasons to stay?

Good old pros versus cons lists help gain insight – only if you're super honest with yourself and dig deeper than a few obvious answers. Even when one list is longer than the other, you get to decide which side is weightier and means more in making the best decision for you.

How much give and take are involved in this project?

Because I like to help people and want to make the world a better place, I'll often put my needs on the back burner. That needs to change. Years ago, I cut out relationships in my life that weren't equal parts of give and take. I have recently realized the same can happen while working on projects. Knowing my worth is recognizing that I deserve to receive and not just give until it hurts in work situations.

Have I tried everything I can to make this work?

I know myself well enough to know that it's hard for me to give up if I feel I've left any stones unturned. Sometimes there are lessons to be learned and growth to be achieved by trying to work things out. Are there boundaries I haven't upheld? Have I clearly communicated my expectations?

As a graduate of the School of Hard Knocks, I've also learned that "making things work" isn't always up to me. People can be toxic, and if I don't have the support of the other people in the equation, there is no way I can succeed. So if what I've tried doesn't seem to make any difference and still isn't good enough, I know it's not about me, and I have to let go.

Do I feel like I'm losing my mind?

Another lesson I learned from the Hard Knock Academy is that when I'm around toxic people and situations, I start to feel like I'm having an out-of-body experience. My brain gets foggy, and I question my judgment. I'm beginning to realize this feeling happens when a trigger from past trauma pops up before I even know what's happening. Thankfully I can recognize this feeling that I'm going crazy as a red flag now and realize that I'm in an unhealthy situation that I must step away from immediately.

What does my body say?

Our bodies really do have a mind of their own and have so much to tell us if we listen. My body has learned that being subtle doesn't work with me, and it has to send a strong message that I can't ignore to let me know something needs to give.

Because I hold tension in my throat, I have problems swallowing when I get super-duper stressed. When this first started, I went to three different doctors to find out what was happening. They all told me nothing was wrong and that it was stress. So now I know that when I can't swallow, it's time to make a change.

Sometimes a break is in order

What do I really want out of my life?

I just celebrated a birthday, so this question is on my mind. I still have so many things I want to do with my life, but I've finally realized that my time on this earth is finite. Making a list of the top four projects I want to make a reality with the time I have left helps me prioritize what I want to get done. Losing focus on where I want my journey to take me makes it easy to get lost along the way, allowing someone else's priority to become my project and wasting my precious time.

How will I let go?

Knowing it's time to let go and actually making changes are two different things. Whether you're rethinking a friendship, marriage, job, or community service, continuing to do something you don't enjoy only makes you miserable. Martyrdom doesn't look good on anyone.

It's okay to cut back, though there will be people who won't be happy about it. The guilt of letting others down is powerful, but it may also be a sign that you've let others become too dependent on you.

Depending on how entrenched you are, it may take some time to orchestrate your departure. Sometimes the best way to quit is to take baby steps. Sometimes the right way to leave is to run screaming down the street. Take some time to sit in stillness and consider your options rather than act rashly or in anger. It helps me to write everything out because as I'm writing, more answers come to me so I can make a dignified plan before I act.

This really is all about you.

Quitting takes bravery. It's scary to make a decision and act on it to step out into the unknown. But I've found that every time I've broken the yoke to run free, it feels like a lifetime of weight has been taken off my shoulders.

No one ever said you have to continue what you're doing forever. Just because you start something doesn't mean the responsibility can't be passed to someone else or put aside to free you to create another fabulous something new.

Remember, this is your life, and it really is all about you. It's time to let go of what is expected of you and live *YOUR* life.

What important criteria will be in your rubric to create an objective tool you can use to know when it's time to let go?

Celebrating Women

Celebrating women artists at the
Finishing School
Poster by Jamie Ford Keiter

It seems incredible that less than 100 years ago, a married woman didn't have the right to own property or sign a contract. She had no right to her wages and no custodial right to children she'd birthed, things we take entirely for granted today. On August 26 each year, we celebrate Women's Equality Day to celebrate women getting the right to vote, a momentous event that started to change these laws.

It wasn't until 1920, after a grueling 70-year battle, that the 19th Amendment was passed, giving white women the right to vote. It wasn't until much later, in fact, 46 years later, in 1966, that women of color were allowed to vote. It's just been since 1971 that people aged 18 to 21 could exercise this right. I've often become frustrated that things aren't changing fast enough for women, that we're still having to fight for wage equity, a presence in the C-Suite, and government offices. I can't imagine the tenacity it took to get one of our most significant rights – the right to vote and the power to have some say over our own lives. Unfortunately, we have to continue to fight to keep these rights.

Lucretia Mott, Elizabeth Cady Stanton, and other early pioneers of the women's rights movement organized the first conference in 1848 in Seneca Falls, New York. They passed the Declaration of Sentiments at that meeting, modeled after the Declaration of Independence. Reading this Declaration today, I realize how it still applies.

The forward-thinking people that drafted and narrowly passed this resolution realized the most crucial issue in this document was the right to vote. To "demand equal station," "absolute tyranny over women" would have to change. One of the things that had to change was that women were expected to "submit to laws, in the formation of which she had no voice." Without this voice, nothing could change, and getting the right to vote became the movement's primary goal.

When you look over the timeline of when different groups of people have received or had their right to vote removed, it's obvious this has to do with power. People in power don't want to give up their position, so allowing people to vote changes things in the most authoritative way possible. Change never happens without a fight. It takes strong people who speak up and stand together in the grueling struggles for change. We can't wait for people to hand us our rights. We have to work together for them continually.

Just as our foremothers knew, voting is one of the most impactful ways to stand up for our beliefs and create change toward equality. By helping choose who makes the laws, we can put people in office that promise to represent our interests. Voting is one of the most important things we can do as citizens, even when we don't like absolutely everything about the candidates.

Rather than giving up this important right, look into which candidate most closely aligns with your values, no matter what party they represent. Placing a vote makes a huge difference in our lives locally and nationally in ways that may not always be obvious. Unfortunately, as we have seen in many elections, races are won or lost by a small number of votes.

Make sure you're registered to vote.

If you haven't voted before or in a while, don't fret. It's easy to register, and this is a great time to start. In most states, you can register online or print out a form and mail it in. Then, if you've moved, changed your name, or want to change your party affiliation, you simply re-register. Easy, peasy! Check with your state's official, secure voting site if you don't know if you're registered, where to vote, or what district you're in.

Research the candidates.

It can be a lot of work to research the truth about what the candidates stand for. The political ads are starting to ramp up, some containing lies meant to scare us into or out of voting for particular candidates. The 411 Voter Guide, put together by the League of Women Voters, lets you put in your address and learn more about who will be on your ballet, biographical information on candidates, and their answers to specific questions. There's a lot more information on this site about where you can meet the candidates, check your registration and polling place, register to vote, and more. It's kind of a one-stop-shopping for all things election.

VOTE!

It's great to get more people registered, but it doesn't mean a thing unless we actually cast a ballot. According to a recent article about our expectations of elected officials, I learned that in the 2019 August state primaries, only 23.2 percent of registered voters in Kansas even bothered to vote. This number of votes was a considerable improvement from the 2017 primaries when only 8.4 percent voted.

It may be easy to ignore these statistics because, traditionally, fewer people vote during primaries. But, the number that showed up to vote in the actual 2017 general election was only 8.3 percent, less than what showed up for the primary! And that's just registered voters. Pew Institute estimates that 21.4 percent of the population doesn't register to vote.

Need a ride?

I like to vote in person at my polling place on Election Day. It's like a neighborhood party, and I always see friends there. Bonus: You get the "I voted" sticker and maybe a cookie too. But, one of the big reasons people don't vote is because they can't get to their polling place. Around the election, there are usually websites that help find a ride to the polls if you need one. Lyft often gives 50 percent off coupons for rides to the polls. Ask a friend for a ride if you need help.

Need an alternative?

Maybe Election Day isn't a good day for you to vote, or it's hard to get away. No worries! There are alternatives to voting on Election Day. You can vote in advance or by mail. You can even vote early in person. There are so many ways to vote. There's really no excuse.

Get involved.

There are many ways to stand up for your beliefs and help spread the word. Research and join a group to volunteer or work for a specific candidate or political party. There are so many ways you can help and so much work to be done.

Do something!

It saddens me what low percentage of people in the United States participate in elections, especially considering how long and hard the fight for the right to vote was and how many people sacrificed so much to win and keep it. We owe it to them to do the easy thing and get off our keisters to put a mark on a ballot. It is more important now than ever to make your voice heard.

What will you do to celebrate our foremothers by taking action around getting more people to vote?

Taking a Stand

The Women's March has brought women together to take a stand

Taking a stand for causes you're passionate about is essential. Rather than sitting around complaining about the state of the world, it is up to us to do something about it. Taking a stand helps make our community a better place for everyone to live.

Becoming active in causes you believe in will give you new insights into people and issues and transform how you see the world. It expands our empathy, giving us a better understanding of how other people live, think, and struggle. Nothing helps you own your power more than standing up for something you strongly believe in.

Activating around a cause doesn't necessarily have to be political. If politics aren't your pet project, there are many other ways to make a difference. I have friends who are active in animal rescue, women's issues, holistic health, promoting the arts, and helping children and people with disabilities. The list goes on and on. You have to find what makes your heart sing and go for it. Or, what chaps your hide? If "these kids today" are making you lose hope in tomorrow, volunteer to tutor at a high school or find a way to mentor young people. Just do something!

All causes you choose to support need your help on an ongoing basis. There are so many issues that it's hard to know where to start. Trying to do too much for too many causes will burn you out quickly, so it's best to choose your battles wisely. Know your limits and do what you can without overwhelming yourself. I heard an interesting suggestion. Rather than trying to do everything, choose one action to be a leader on, one action to be a follower for, and one action to make a habit.

To be realistic about life, there will be some causes we're passionate about that we'll just have to let others attend to. That's okay. As an overachiever, I've realized I'm just one person and can't do it all by myself. It's selfish even to think I can. Set a boundary for yourself by deciding how much time, on average, per week you can dedicate yourself to help. Setting a schedule will help you budget your time to determine how involved you can be and how many causes you can support.

Here are some other tips for you.

Fighting for Women

Join an established organization and volunteer.

Look for local organizations that are already established and get involved. If you can give one hour of your time a week, that's 52 hours a year that you've worked to make a difference. Even the busiest people can manage that.

Donate.

Giving money to organizations that work on causes you care about is a simple way to make a big difference. Research organizations you plan to give money to or raise funds for, so you know where your money will go and what it will pay for.

If you see something, do something.

No matter what it is, if you see something that doesn't look right, do something. Take videos on your phone and share them. Report harassment, whether you or someone else is the victim. Get help to rescue animals in danger. Pick up litter you see in your path. Every little bit makes a difference somewhere.

Offer moral support to vocal friends.

Working on causes can be frustrating, hard work. Help keep hard-working people motivated by checking in on your active friends, thanking them for their hard work, and encouraging them to keep going. Let them know they're not alone. Be an ally for friends who deal with oppression. Remember to take care of yourself as well. You can't advocate if you ignore your health.

Speak your truth.

No matter which causes you fight for, don't let anyone convince you that you don't have a voice and that what you have to say isn't valid or important. There will always be people who don't have the same priorities and opinions. It is perfectly acceptable to agree to disagree. However, it is not acceptable to take away others' rights to be heard, even when we disagree. Most importantly – ignore the trolls.

Let your money talk.

Deciding which companies to do business with, based on their business practices and to whom they give charitable contributions, sends a powerful message. Research the companies you spend money with to determine what and who they support. I love the Goods Unite Us app on my phone to check out who I want to spend my hard-earned cash spendolas with.

Do your research.

When stories support our views, it's especially easy to get pulled into sensationalist websites that are in business to make money from advertising, not reporting the facts. To ensure the news is accurate, do some research before sharing by searching for other articles on the same topic to determine if the site is reputable.

Call your elected officials.

No matter what your cause, the most effective way to let elected officials know where you stand is by writing and calling them. If you're not sure what to say or don't feel confident about making the call, do some research and script out a statement that's short, sweet, and to the point.

Vote!

One of our most significant responsibilities as citizens is to let our voice be heard by voting in every election. Take time to find out your representatives' platforms, rather than voting for one party, to find the candidates that best align with your beliefs. Don't skip primaries and local elections. They are just as important, if not more so than national elections.

What action will you take?

What Are Your Superpowers?

Wonder Woman is my role model. I became a super fan of this superhero when I was 14 years old, and the Wonder Woman series with Lynda Carter debuted.

Watching a woman running around rescuing people, fighting evil, and kicking ass thrilled me. It was such a departure from the typical damsel in distress storyline. It was surprising, and it made me think, "Why couldn't a woman be a superhero? We can do anything!"

I love the story of how Wonder Woman came to be. Psychologist Willian Moulton Marston, the inventor of the blood pressure test and the polygraph machine, conducted many experiments to discover women are fundamentally more honest than men and that the future of humankind lay in the hands of women. Recognizing comic books as a way to influence people, Marston created a female answer to Superman, representing what he considered feminine values of kindness and compassion without being seen as weak.

I draw deep inspiration from this character and what she embodies for me:

- A woman who owns her power and uses it for good, not evil.
- She is a fighter for those who can't fight for themselves and never gives up in her battle for justice.
- She can stop a war with love.
- She has empathy for people and animals.

Wonder Woman is not just a fictional character. Wonder Woman is a mindset.

In getting ready for a presentation I have coming up, I've been thinking and researching superpowers and how we can discover what ours are. I've come to believe that we can hone our values, passions, talents, and strengths into superpowers when we determine what these traits are.

Values

The principles or values we hold at our core are what guide us through life. Knowing what we stand for is powerful. Defining the ideals we stand for reduces unfortunate choices and regrets, helping to make decisions we can live with and keeping us on track to become the person we want to be.

It takes some deep introspection to decide which values you want your life to represent. So, to help you get started, take out some paper and markers and get star-struck:

- Who do you admire most, and *why*?
- Who are your heroes (past or present), and what is it that you admire most about them?
- Who or what inspires you?

By studying the values that you admire in others, you'll uncover the qualities that are *also* in you, whether you're aware of them or not. Now that you have a list of the traits you admire, choose three or four that you can hold dear and use as a guiding star for your life.

While it may seem that coming up with a grocery list of words rather than a few will make you stronger, having too many choices diffuses focus and makes decisions more complicated. Besides, three or four principles are challenging enough to live by. For nearly 80 years, Wonder Woman has stood as a symbol for truth, justice, and equality, which seems more than enough to keep Diane and her golden lariat busy.

Passion

Passion is powerful. It is the driving force that fuels and inspires us to keep reaching for our goals, no matter how lofty the ambition or questionably sane they may be. Passion brings color and meaning into our lives and impacts happiness, excitement, anticipation, and success.

So many people struggle with figuring out their passions as if knowing this opens up some kind of magical door that leads to a fulfilled life. We have our entire lives to discover our passion and find new ones. The problem with finding your passion is that we try to use our heads to define what we desire when the answers can only be found in our hearts. What makes your heart sing?

Make a list of everything that you love about life.

- Who do you love most in your life and why?
- What are the qualities that make you sparkle when you see them?
- What activities do you absolutely *love* to do?

Add as many items to this list as possible, then look at your list to see if you can spot any common themes. Our deepest *passions* are often concealed within the things we love most.

Talents

Our natural abilities, or talents, are hard-wired into us from birth. These abilities are intuitive and come to us easily, which is what makes talent different from knowledge and skills. Talents help us understand our strengths are often a result of our passions and years and years of practice.

Keep an open mind while identifying your talents. Our abilities come in all shapes and sizes, extending to many areas of life beyond the ability to play the accordion or dance like Ginger Rogers. For example, the gift of gab can be a handy talent. Here are more questions to get you started:

- What are you known for? What do people compliment you about?
- What comes naturally and effortlessly to you? What activities make you lose track of time?
- What have you loved to do since you were a wee one?
- What do you know a lot about? What do you think about?

Don't hold back on your list of talents. Even if you think the talent is unimportant, list it! Then, when you finish, refine your inventory a bit to combine like skills and look for patterns. Unlike core values, you can have many talents to develop!

Strengths

Cultivating our strengths, rather than trying to convert "weaknesses," saves time. By taking the focus off the negative, we move closer to finding our superpowers rather than our kryptonite. Don't limit your thinking as to what counts as a strength. Consider relationships, resources, and reputation, as well as your skills and abilities.

To gauge your strengths, a good place to start is by looking at your gold star moments, like these:

- Make a list of things you've been successful at throughout your life.
- What accomplishments in your life are you most proud of?

· What am I doing or talking about when I feel the most energized and happy?

Beyond looking for your strengths, determine which skills are worthy of building. For example, just because you're good at playing the kazoo doesn't mean you need to start training for the Philharmonic. It's also important to realize that you can develop new strengths with life experience, just like passion and talents.

Putting it all together

When you've defined your values, passions, talents, and strengths, write them down, side by side, to see what comes up.

· What patterns do you see?
· Are there any concepts that overlap between the categories?
· Can you see how ideas build off each other to work together?

Putting all the columns together is where the magic happens. Here's an example of what I found in my life:

Core Value	Passion	Talent	Strength
Love	Helping people grow	Gift of gab Creativity	Teaching Writing

From looking at the patterns, it's evident that one of my superpowers is being the Headmistress of the Finishing School for Modern Women! My core values and passion are why I've taken on such an endeavor. My talents are the abilities I had to get started, and my strengths have grown as I've flexed my talent muscles in my role as Headmistress.

Core values help us navigate which path is right for our life. Passions lead us to the purpose we are destined for. Our talents and the strengths we develop will help us achieve the spiritual and life goals we need for a fulfilling life. It only makes sense that our superpowers are a combination of these attributes.

In the words of Lynda Carter, "Our number one job is to honor the goddess within! Your secret self is a true Wonder Woman...so let her shine!"

What are your superpowers?

You are a superhero!

Join us!

I'd love to hear from you!

There are questions at the end of each essay that I hope you'll spend some brain cells thinking over. Writing down your answers has even more power to anchor your thoughts and turn them into reality. Write in this book or in a special, fabulous journal you select to be your Never Finished journey or digitize it on an electronic device.

Doing this homework has extra rewards. Send me an email at jill@finishingschoolformodernwomen.com with the subject line "Here's my homework!" and I'll send you a special surprise.

Another way to get a special surprise is to let me know what you think of this book. Use the subject line "Thoughts" at the same email address.

Finishing School
for
MODERN WOMEN

Join our community!

Go to our website at www.finishingschoolformodern-women.com and click Join Us. You'll become part of our community, interacting with women near and far to share thoughts, insights, ideas, resources, accomplishments, and so much more. You'll also get notifications when I post a new blog. Bringing women together to learn from each other is what the Finishing School for Modern Women is all about. Don't be shy. We're excited to get to know you!

Much love!
Headmistress Jill

Acknowledgements

This book would never have happened without the support of a lot of people.

Thank you to everyone who has supported the Finishing School for Modern Women. Your attention to life-long learning keeps the flow of ideas coming and the motivation to keep writing week after week.

Thanks to Jen Sincero for the inspiration to turn my blogs into a book of essays. Reading her Badass books and seeing Jen speak in person convinced me am worthy of achieving this monumental goal and the importance of speaking my voice.

Thank you to the team of women who helped me shape my work, brand, thinking, and life. No one can do it alone, and I'm grateful you were along for the ride. Cecilia Rogers, Rebecca Morris, Jamie Ford-Keiter, you are my secret weapon.

Special appreciation to Jessica Wasson-Crook, my brand manager, book cover designer, millennial mentor, enthusiastic cheerleader, and life-long friend. Thank you for your loving support, sometimes through a kick in the pants.

Thanks to all the advisors and editors that helped me get this book ready to release into the wild. Sarah Bagby, Cecilia Green, Teri Mott, Shannon Littlejohn, Cecilia Rogers, and Mandy Sykes, your guidance, insights, and editorial expertise helped me polish this work so there are fewer problems for our grammarian friends to find.

Thank you to my family, friends, and mentors. I am who I am because of your encouragement to reach for the stars. You've helped me explore who I am, given me advice and leadership when I needed you, and the love and acceptance to be my bona fide freaky self.

Special appreciation to my mom, Cecilia Green, for being my mentor, editor, co-conspirator, and role model. You encouraged my love of the arts and nurtured my skills as a writer. This book happened because of your push to let my light shine.

Finally, thank you to all the women's rights activists and advocates for setting the way. If it weren't for you, the Finishing School for Modern Women would be centered around social graces and attracting husbands than finding our authentic selves and stepping into our power.

www.ingramcontent.com/pod-product-compliance
Lightning Source LLC
Chambersburg PA
CBHW032052020426
42335CB00011B/307